Book Banning in 21st-Century America

Beta Phi Mu Scholars

Founded in 1948, Beta Phi Mu is the international library and information studies honor society. Its mission is to recognize and encourage scholastic achievement among library and information studies students. The Beta Phi Mu Scholars series publishes significant contributions and substantive advances in the field of library and information science. Series editor Lorraine Haricombe and associate editor Keith Russell are committed to presenting work which reflects Beta Phi Mu's commitments to scholarship, leadership, and service. The series fosters creative, innovative, and well-articulated works that members of the field will find influential.

Recently Published Titles in the Series

Book Banning in 21st-Century America by Emily J. M. Knox

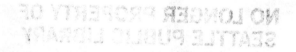

Book Banning in 21st-Century America

Emily J. M. Knox

ROWMAN & LITTLEFIELD
Lanham • Boulder • New York • London

Published by Rowman & Littlefield
An imprint of The Rowman & Littlefield Publishing Group, Inc.
4501 Forbes Boulevard, Suite 200, Lanham, Maryland 20706
www.rowman.com

86-90 Paul Street, London EC2A 4NE

British Library Cataloguing in Publication Information Available

Library of Congress Cataloging-in-Publication Data

Knox, Emily, 1976–
Book banning in 21st-century America / Emily J. M. Knox.
pages cm. – (Beta Phi Mu scholars)
Includes bibliographical references and index.
ISBN 978-1-4422-3167-2 (cloth) – ISBN 978-1-5381-7112-7 (paperback) –
ISBN 978-1-4422-3168-9 (ebook)
1. Public libraries–Censorship–United States. 2. School libraries–Censorship–United
States. 3. Challenged books–United States. 4. Intellectual freedom–United States. 5.
Books and reading–United States. I. Title.
Z711.4.K65 2015 303.3'76–dc23 2014036356

Preface

At the beginning of the 21st century, an incredible assortment of media including books are readily available to anyone with a computer, tablet, smartphone, and an Internet connection, so what is the point of trying to ban a book from the public library or remove it from the school curriculum? This book attempts to provide some answers to this question. I have long been interested in exploring the reasons why people challenge books. My mother was a high school media specialist for over 30 years and she would bring home Banned Books Week literature every year and encouraged me to write my book reports on frequently challenged books. Books that I loved, like Judy Blume's *Are You There God? It's Me, Margaret*, appeared on the list every year. What were people trying to accomplish trying to remove or restrict these books? What did they think would happen if I read them?

Unlike a lot of research on intellectual freedom and censorship, which tends to focus on bibliography, ethics, and policy, *Book Banning in 21st-Century America* explores the arguments of the challengers themselves. These arguments are often dismissed in both the general and professional media, but I believe that by taking challengers' justifications for their actions seriously, information professionals can be better prepared for challenges to materials in their collections. *Book Banning* is based on research that I initially completed for my dissertation. Over the four years since the initial study I have added three cases to the analysis, and there are additional interviews, public hearings, and documentary data. One of the most difficult aspects of the study was finding challengers who were willing to be interviewed, and I am grateful to all who agreed to speak to someone on the "other side." This study would not have the same resonance without their thoughtful answers to my questions.

As stated throughout the book, the practices of censorship demonstrate the relationship between knowledge and power. The study presented here focuses on the discourse of challengers particularly with regard to their understanding of the effects of knowledge and how they use their symbolic power to control access to certain cultural materials within public institutions. Through analysis of challengers' discourse, we can more clearly understand the connection between knowledge and power and also provide better responses to those who attempt to remove, restrict, and relocate materials.

As a former professional librarian, I should note that I am not neutral on the issue of censorship, although I have attempted to adopt a neutral tone. I strongly support the ALA's policies on intellectual freedom and work to uphold them in my academic and professional life. In some respects, this makes me a direct antagonist to people who bring challenges against books. However, what unites me and the challengers is our belief that reading is powerful. Books change lives. With this in mind, I endeavored throughout this study to be open to challengers' arguments and not impose my own biases on their own worldviews concerning books and reading.

Acknowledgments

There are many people I would like to thank for their support through this project. My parents, Jo Emily and Nathaniel Knox, have always lovingly supported me in all my endeavors. My friends and colleagues in central New Jersey and central Illinois are the best. I would especially like to thank Amani Ayad, Monica Carr, Nicole Cooke, Steve Di Domenico, Sam Hack, Derek Hoiem, Jeff Putney, Camille Reyes, Patrick Rietz, John Sanders, and Gergana Slavova. Thank you to my editors at Rowman & Littlefield, Charles Harmon and Lara Graham, for keeping the project moving along. I cannot overstate my gratitude to everyone who agreed to be interviewed for this study. This work would not be the same without your willingness to speak to me. My advisor, Marija Dalbello, for providing wonderful guidance throughout the dissertation stage of this project. Gratitude and hugs to Simon Lawrence, Kyle Peppers, and Nancy Friedrich for our approximately 10, 20, and 30 years of friendship, respectively.

Finally, I would like to thank Yolanda Sotelo for the photo on the cover of the book. It was taken just before the books from the Tucson Unified School District Mexican American Studies program were sent to the local textbook depository. Although the Tucson case is not part of the main analysis in the book, the picture vividly captures the consequences of banning books in the United States.

Chapter One

Trusting the System

AT THE BOARD MEETING

I'm not quite sure where I'm going. Traffic on the Garden State Parkway was heavy and now I'm running late. The school is huge and I'm supposed to find my way to the cafeteria, but somehow I've opened the door to the gym. There's a basketball game in progress and I have to walk around it with many eyes on me as the players travel up and down the court. Several wrong turns later I find the cafeteria and it is packed. The board is sitting at tables in the front of the room, and almost every chair intended for attendees is taken. I suspect that this is not a normal turnout for the Westfield (New Jersey) School Board Meeting. About two weeks prior, a parent challenged *The Absolutely True Diary of a Part-Time Indian* by Sherman Alexie for its inclusion in the school district's high school English curriculum, and many community members have come to the meeting to voice their opinions on this development. The mood is fairly neutral as I take a seat at the back of the audience and turn on my recorder.

As in many board meetings, this one begins with a call for comments on the agenda. A man who had been sitting directly in front of me jumps up and walks quickly to the microphone: "When did the board first become aware that this book is in this curriculum?" It is clear that he has misunderstood the request and is asked to sit down as comments on the book will come later on the agenda. The mood in the room immediately changes—the atmosphere is suddenly much more tense than before. The man who went to the podium has returned to his seat and is constantly fidgeting. He has a copy of the book with him, many of its pages marked by paper clips. Another attendee taps him on the shoulder and they go out into the hallway, presumably to discuss the book.

Much to the dismay of most of the attendees (including myself), prior to public comment there is a long presentation on technology upgrades for the district. The crowd gets a bit restless during the 35-minute presentation, and the man who spoke earlier mutters, "Jesus H. Christ" in the middle. After a 25-minute discussion and comment session, we have finally reached the challenged book agenda item. The board members and administration speak first. Dr. Margaret Dolan, the school superintendent, gives the history of the complaint, noting that the book went through a full vetting process including reviews by district committees. Then members of the Curriculum and Policy Committees give their reports, noting that members of both committees discussed the book several times and also reviewed the vetting process for curriculum materials.

By this point, 15 minutes have passed and the attendees are starting to get restless. Finally, it is time for public comments on the book. The first few speakers, some of whom are students, all offer support for the book and the board's decision to retain it in the curriculum. The fifth speaker's testimony is notable as she does not focus on problems with the book itself but asks that the book be classified as optional reading for students. "As far as the parents are concerned," she says, "this issue is not about book banning but about parents' rights, accountability transparency, and trust in our public school system." The board president and superintendent both reply to the speaker, saying that they did follow procedures for reevaluating the book.

The next speaker is the original letter writer. She is a bit hesitant as she notes that her neighbors have called her names. She insists that her complaint is not about removing the book permanently but figuring how books are chosen for the curriculum in the first place: "This is not about banning. It is about being selective and the process used to determine the selection." She also states that she no longer trusts the system:

> I still don't know how the department head was completely unaware of this book and I am surprised to learn that any teacher can bring a book into a school district without board approval. I still feel that I'm not completely in trust of the system and I really would like to regain that trust. And I would like to work together to address this problem to prevent it from happening again in the future.

She notes that, for her, Alexie's book crosses the line into indecency and the fact that the district would require students to read such a "controversial" book means that it has lowered the bar for obscenity in school.

The man who jumped up during the request for comments on the agenda is the next speaker. "Leaving everything up to the schools is crazy!" he growls. The speaker is clearly angry, and the crowd responds verbally and the president of the board bangs his gavel. Things settle down a bit but it is clear from the response of the crowd that this book challenge has caused a rift in the community. Everyone is learning things about their neighbors and local institutions that they previously didn't know. Some of the neighbors are "censors" who want to keep realistic fiction away from youth while others are "permissive" and will allow their children to read anything. Some believe that the school is helping students learn about "diversity" while others think it is allowing students to read "lewd" material. After a few more speakers the comment period ends and, even though there is more on the meeting agenda, almost all the attendees leave the meeting. Eventually—though not that night—the board would vote to retain the book.

The Westfield case was one of 464 book challenges that, according to statistics from the American Library Association's (ALA) Office for Intellectual Freedom (OIF), took place across the country in 2012. Between 2000 and 2013, the OIF logged 6,544 challenges in all 50 states.[1] The association estimates that, for every challenge that is reported, approximately four or five challenges go unrecorded. Even though this is common practice, little is known about the people who bring these challenges. In the mass media, they are often categorized by the media as "concerned citizens" or "concerned parents," but there has been little empirical research on their overall motivations except in the broadest terms. In fact, the challengers in New Jersey are the latest in a long line of groups and individuals who use their social and symbolic power to curb access to cultural goods. The citizens used their power, as taxpayers and parents, over the local school district to attempt to block access to knowledge that they considered to be illicit. However, there is something odd about this attempt to keep students from reading *The Absolutely True Diary of a Part-Time Indian*. If someone wants to read Alexie's book it is available in the local public library, it can be bought on Amazon (in several different formats), one can order it through interlibrary loan, or illegally download it on any number of torrent sites. If the book is so readily available, what are these community members trying to accomplish? In order to better understand the actions of the challengers in Westfield, which for expediency I will call "book banning," it is necessary to situate book challenges within the history and practice of censorship in the West.

BOOK CHALLENGES AND CENSORSHIP: CONCEPTS AND CONTEXTS

Book challenges are requests by members of the public to remove, relocate, or restrict books from or within institutions. Relocating books includes such practices as moving books from the open shelves in the children's section to the open shelves in the adult section or placing books "behind the desk." Restricting means that users cannot access a particular book without parental permission or that there are age restrictions placed on the circulation policy for the book. If the book is removed as a result of the request, it is then considered to be "banned" and is not accessible to anyone—regardless of age—who wishes to read it. Although some might argue that the latter practice of removal is the only true instance of "censorship," it should be noted that both relocation and restriction restrict user access to information. If someone must ask a staff member for a book or the book is not in the expected place (e.g., it is in the adult section of the library instead of the young adult section), the information contained within the book is no longer readily accessible to the reader who wants it. Of course, this outcome is precisely what the challengers intend.

It is clear, even from the brief definitions given above, that censorship is a contested term. Censorship, broadly understood, refers to control over the production and distribution of texts and other cultural goods. While some might argue that only governments can censor, others argue that anyone, including groups and individuals, can impede the creation and circulation of goods. The latter definition is often characterized as a broad conceptualization of censorship while the former is a narrow definition of the practice.[2] In order to more fully explore these two conceptualizations of the practice of censorship, it is fruitful to view censorship not as a single action but an amalgamation of practices and behaviors that operate within a particular institutional context. For example, within the context of a nation, governments have both the power and resources to impede the creation and distribution of those cultural goods it deems harmful. On a smaller scale, it is possible to curb circulation of certain cultural goods within a particular community by passing local laws through the city council or requesting that such goods be removed from public institutions including schools and libraries. It is this latter practice that is the focus of this book. However, note that in all of these instances, censorship is, to use Sue Curry Jansen's term, the "knot" that combines power and knowledge.[3]

Censorship practices can be either proactive or reactive. Proactive censorship focuses on the creation and production of materials. This is most clearly exemplified by state-sponsored censorship. However, another example might be when librarians, teachers, or administrators choose not to order or teach certain materials because they fear engendering controversy in their communities. Yet another example of proactive censorship is self-censorship on the part of creators and distributors. As will be demonstrated in the analysis chapters, challengers sometimes advocate this practice. Reactive censorship, on the other hand, is focused on distribution or circulation of cultural goods. An example might be the redaction of classified material in a government document or the removal of books from a library shelf or classroom. In all cases, these practices result in reducing the public's access to the cultural good.

CENSORSHIP: HISTORY AND CONTEXT

Although censorship practices have a long history, the current usage of the word is a modern construction. From the term for the Roman office *censor* or "one who monitors morality" according to the *Oxford English Dictionary*, the modern sense of the word relating to the general circulation of information in society dates to the early 19th century. It is not coincidental that this understanding of the term dates to a time of proliferation of texts, broad circulation of knowledge, and rise in literacy rates across the Western world. Along with classifying censorship practices as reactive or proactive, it is also fruitful to view historical and contemporary censorship as following particular types of models. Although used anachronistically, the term "model of censorship" demonstrates how various societal structures, including institutions and individuals, operated within a particular historical framework.

To begin, it is important to stipulate that the flow of information and intricacies of the circulation of texts and other cultural goods are, of course, related to power. In order to be labeled a "censor," governments, groups, or individuals must have sufficient power to exert control over the production or distribution of cultural goods. In the realm of the circulation of written texts, there are cultural and social changes that began in the early modern era that continue to resonate today. The examples below focus on state-sponsored, institutional, and individual censorship.

In the state-sponsored model, the state or its representatives uses its power over both the people and commerce to curb the creation and distribution of written texts. The Roman *censor* mentioned above is one example of this type of state-sponsored censorship. Another example is found in accounts of the distribution of print during the ancien régime of 18th-century France. All works had to be submitted to royal censors and could only be printed if they were endorsed with the royal privilege. That is, the power to censor rested in the institution of the monarchy. In his famous history of the *Encyclopédie* and the print trade, Robert Darnton writes that

> by granting a privilege, the king did not merely allow a book to come into being: he put his stamp of approval on it; he recommended it to his subjects, speaking through one or more censors who expatiated on its importance and even its style in long-winded permissions and approbations that were usually printed in the book along with a formal lettre de privilège from the king. [4]

Here the state in the human form of the king literally puts its imprimatur upon a work in order for it to be published. This model of censorship was also practiced in Great Britain where the state enacted licensing acts for publishers from the 17th through the mid-19th century. According to Julian Petley, it is difficult to measure the efficacy of the acts but is probably that such acts encourage authors to self-censor.[5] It should also be noted that the inherent push and pull between what is acceptable and unacceptable for the reading public is an important aspect of censorship practices throughout history.

One of the most well-known examples of the institutional model, the second model of censorship outlined here, was practiced by the Roman Catholic Church by means of its *Index Librorum Prohibitorum* published between 1559 and 1966. This list of banned books included material that the Vatican considered to be heretical, impure, or obscene. Works by authors including Gustave Flaubert, Emile Zola, George Sand, and Simone de Beauvoir were all listed in the *Index*. According to Peter Burke, the *Index* was an attempt to "fight print with print."[6] Church leaders intended it to be a corrective to both Protestantism and the spread of printing. This is typical of the institutional model wherein a nongovernmental entity uses its influence over members to control access to certain types of knowledge.

The final model of censorship discussed here, and one of the most important for understanding contemporary challenge cases to materials in public institutions in the United States, is associated with a particular individual (or small group of individuals) and his or her influence over society or local community. In contrast to the state-sponsored model of Old Regime France or the institutional model of the Catholic Church, in the United States, censorship is often associated with a particular individual's influence over the wider society or local community rather than the state. However, this is a change that took place over time. One example of a liminal figure in this process is Anthony Comstock, who in the late 19th century used his position as postal inspector to determine which materials would be allowed through U.S. ports.[7] Although his position was part of the government institution, the obscenity laws from this era bear his name and are more associated with his persona rather than the U.S. government. An example of censorship that is not connected to the state is the work of the antivice societies of New York and Boston in the late 19th century who used their social influence to censor museum and library collections.[8] This shift from direct institutional censorship to individuals using the tools of institutions and public opinion to censor is important for understanding the actions and arguments of challengers that are the focus of the study presented here. Challengers wield their power using the tools of state, but their actions are often the work of either one individual or a small group of individuals.

These models aid our understanding of how censorship operates within a given society. The cases in this book are examples of the third model of censorship wherein individuals or groups use their social power and influence to proactively impede access to cultural goods. We can understand book challenges as a practice of individuals who are exercising their rights as citizens of the United States and their influence within their local communities to effect change within local public institutions. It should be noted that these citizens do not have direct control over what gets taught in classrooms or placed in library shelves. They instead use persuasion and argument to convince staff or board members to remove, relocate, or restrict a particular book. These rationalizations might be considered to be one facet of the discourse of censorship that challengers employ to sway decision makers in a particular direction.

THE DISCOURSE OF CENSORSHIP

The discourse of censorship incorporates many different types of discourse. It includes discourses that inform and surround such practices as book burning, state-sponsored filtering of the Internet, and technological antiprivacy measures. As noted earlier, this discourse demonstrates an intimate relationship between knowledge and power. Discourse, as it is used here, operates in two modes. To use Pierre Bourdieu's terms, discourse is a structuring structure that provides the means for people to know and construct objects in the world. [9] That is, it is a framework for cognition. In this first mode, discourse informs how challengers recognize materials that they consider to be "inappropriate." Challengers' understanding of this term often draws on other discourses, including those that inform moral beliefs or constructions of child development. In its second mode, discourse operates as a structured structure that provides signification or meaning to objects in the world. That is, in this mode, the discourse of censorship allows challengers to more fully describe which materials should be removed, restricted, or relocated. Using this framework, discourse is most easily understood as a type of poetic—defined here as the creative practices of individuals that take place within a structured space. Individuals work within both institutionalized structure imposed by librarians and other administrators in public institutions as well as the structures of their own personal worldviews to craft a justification for censorship.

As noted previously, the discourse of censorship has many different facets. Note that while challengers focus on the inappropriateness of certain books and the opaque policies of schools or libraries, other aspects of the discourse of censorship center on other arguments and related discourses regarding the access to information. For example, book burning, while it is also sometimes focused on inappropriate books, is an argument that draws on practices that relate to purging and the cleansing nature of fire. [10] As will be demonstrated in this study, challengers to materials in public institutions in the United States employ discourses that focus on the safety of public institutions, the decline of morality in society, and the nature of reading.

The analysis presented here is most closely related to what Reiner Keller calls culturalist discourse research. [11] Using the sociology of knowledge as a foundation, Keller divides discourse analysis into six types, including the ethics of discourse and corpus linguistics. Culturalist discourse research focuses on symbolic interactionism. Social actors employ both symbolic power (e.g., power as citizens within a given community) and language (terms such as "inappropriate" or "innocent") as a means to affect the distribution of particular types of knowledge. As Keller notes, discourse is a "power struggle or struggle for truth, for symbolic and material ordering of social practices from which historically contingent power knowledge regimes emerge."[12] As the analysis in this book will show, the discourse of censorship and more specifically the discourse of challengers informs a reality wherein only some members of a given community (or nation) should have access to certain types of information while others should be excluded.

PREVIOUS RESEARCH ON CHALLENGERS

As I have noted elsewhere, research in intellectual freedom and censorship tends to fall within five different categories: bibliography, information ethics, policy and procedure, historical case studies, and contemporary case studies.[13] Robert P. Doyle's triennial *Banned Books Resource Guide* (*Banned Books: Challenging Our Freedom to Read*), published by the ALA, is a well-known example of bibliography on censorship. It lists and describes challenge cases throughout the United States.[14] In the area of information ethics, in an article on privacy and Internet access, Alan Rubel uses a framework based on philosophical definitions of negative and positive freedom to argue that intellectual freedom should be understood as a quality of individual agency.[15] Recommendations for policies that public institutions might implement to respond to challenges can be found in the American Library Association's *Intellectual Freedom Manual* and the series "Protecting Intellectual Freedom in Your Library," also published by the association.[16] Historical case studies include book-length histories of specific cases including Louise S. Robbins's *The Dismissal of Miss Ruth Brown* and Shirley A. and Wayne A. Wiegand's *Books on Trial*.[17] The myriad essays in the edited volume *True Stories of Censorship Battles in America's Libraries* offer many examples of contemporary case studies.[18] As noted above, there has been little previous research on challengers. One example of this area of intellectual freedom research is an article from the 1980s in which the authors, Norman Poppel and Edwin M. Ashley, found that censors have two motivations behind their actions: first, they have a high sense of community, and second, one of their primary concerns revolves around the moral development of their children.[19] Note that in the study described in this book, I found both of these motivations within the themes of challengers. Another example of work that focuses on challengers is James LaRue's monograph, *The New Inquisition*. Although it is more of a handbook detailing how institutions should respond to challengers, LaRue does note that challengers are often motivated by a mission to ensure that the institutions (the public library in this case) is in keeping with the challengers' worldviews and that they are in "awe of the written word."[20] As will be demonstrated throughout the book, these were also common themes in the discourse of challengers analyzed in this study.

Two recent dissertations in library and information science (LIS) also provide empirical analysis of challengers' arguments. The first, by Kelly Kingrey, explores how conservative Christian groups understand the terms "intellectual freedom" and "censorship" and how these concepts are related to their definitions of rights and responsibilities.[21] The second dissertation, by Loretta Gaffney, uses reader-response theory to explore how conservative social groups understand the importance of public libraries in communities, the practice of reading, and the meaning of access to information.[22] The study presented here employs some of the methods and findings from these two dissertations to analyze the discourse of individual challengers who try to remove, relocate, or restrict access to materials in public institutions. In particular, Kingrey's findings regarding how conservative Christians define intellectual freedom and censorship aided in the analysis of challengers' arguments regarding the impact of their actions on readers while Gaffney's use of reader-response theory informs the analysis of how challengers understand the effects of reading.

The study presented here focuses on how book challengers employ the language of social decay and the effects of reading to exert their symbolic power as members and citizens of a particular community over its public institutions as a means of curtailing others' access to certain cultural materials. Unlike many investigations in intellectual freedom and censorship, some of which are described above, the study focuses on the arguments of challengers themselves rather than the books that are challenged.[23] The study's primary purpose was to better understand some common aspects of the worldviews of people who challenge books in public libraries, school libraries, and classrooms. The method of analysis, rooted in social constructionism, the theory of practice, and print culture studies, focuses on the common themes within the discourse of these challengers. In particular, the study identifies the challengers' understanding of the state of contemporary American society and their construction of the role of public institutions in this society, as well as their understanding of the practice of reading.

Most importantly, this study takes up Wayne Wiegand's call for LIS researchers to study the practice of reading.[24] It investigates a little-researched group, those who challenge materials, whose actions have great import on the information professions.[25] The study views the discourse of censorship employed by challengers as essentially a discourse about society and the importance of reading. By gaining a deeper understanding of how challengers conceptualize the practice of reading, librarians and information professionals can better understand why challenge cases are brought against materials in the first place. In order to provide a foundation for understanding the context for the study, a few key terms are defined below.

KEY TERMS AND BACKGROUND

When book challenges are initiated, it is not unusual for the local media to cover the story. These news items often focus on the book in question and the status of the individual or group that brings the challenge. For example, in the *Seattle Times*, the challenger is introduced as a mother who "took issue" with Aldous Huxley's *Brave New World*.[26] Terms such as "banning" and "censorship" are often used loosely to describe many different types of censorship practices including challenges, removal, and restriction. However, these terms often depend on one's point of view regarding a particular context or situation and are therefore highly political. In light of this, terms and concepts used throughout the study are defined below.

Intellectual Freedom

This study investigates how the actions of individuals, through the use of their symbolic power over public institutions, can restrict the intellectual freedom of other individuals. Although the term "intellectual freedom" is rarely used by challengers, this concept permeates much of the discourse of censorship. Intellectual freedom is best understood as an ontological state that encompasses two distinct circumstances: First, that individuals have the right to a belief and to express that belief. Second, that society is committed to allowing access to information by all.[27] In the United States, the roots of support for intellectual freedom are based in the utilitarian philosophy of John Stuart Mill, whose treatise *On Liberty* argues that in order to know that one's beliefs are correct, it is imperative to hear the arguments of those who disagree with you. Mill offers four grounds for the freedom of expression. First, that some oppressed opinions may be true. Second, that such opinions, even if they are false, may hold some grain of truth. Next, that truth must be contested or it is simply prejudiced opinion, and, finally, that one's truths must be held with conviction from both reason and personal experience.[28] This philosophical framework for intellectual freedom became more widespread in the 20th century and is codified in international policy in Articles 18 and 19 of the United Nations Declaration of Human Rights.[29]

Many organizations and scholars have defined intellectual freedom over the years. As a major supporter of an individual's right to intellectual freedom in the United States, the American Library Association provides a straightforward definition for the term: "Intellectual freedom is the right of every individual to both seek and receive information from all points of view without restriction. It provides for free access to all expressions of ideas through which any and all sides of a question, cause, or movement may be explored."[30] This definition is clear; however, one might argue that it is somewhat narrow and overly focused on information transmission. In her article on the state of intellectual freedom research in the early 21st century, Eliza Dresang provides another definition, stating that it is the "freedom to think or believe what one will, freedom to express one's thought and beliefs in unrestricted manners and means, and freedom to access information and ideas regardless of the content or viewpoints of the author(s) or the age, background, or beliefs of the receiver."[31] This definition is more expansive than the one put forth by the American Library Association and highlights freedom of thought, belief, and expression.

In this study, intellectual freedom is defined as a right to access the whole of the information universe without fear of reprisal from the "powers that be." This definition approaches intellectual freedom as a social justice issue and is based on the work of Peter Lor and Johannes Britz.[32] Following from their work in their native South Africa, Lor and Britz argue that knowledge societies cannot exist without freedom of access to information and that impeding the distribution of information ultimately leads to corruption of institutions, including the state.

Types of Knowledge

Although intellectual freedom is broadly concerned with many different types of speech, knowledge, and ideas, this study is primarily concerned with the classification of knowledge and how accessible these are to various classes of people. According to Burke, different types of knowledge can be classified as dichotomous pairs: theoretical knowledge is commonly paired with and against practical knowledge while high and low, liberal and useful, as well as specialized and universal also form dichotomous pairs of knowledge.[33] For this study, two such dichotomous pairs of knowledge are particularly relevant to understanding challenge cases. First, public and private knowledge concern, respectively, knowledge known to all and knowledge that is limited to only a few. The delineation between legitimate and forbidden knowledge is also salient for understanding challenge cases. Forbidden knowledge is *arcana Dei*, or knowledge for God alone, and stands against legitimate knowledge, which can be known by all. Challenge cases often focus on whether or not particular knowledge should be classified as public or legitimate and whether or not certain groups of people are granted the intellectual freedom to access such knowledge. Another model for classifying knowledge is discussed by Kerry H. Robinson in her work on the social construction of knowledge and "difficult" knowledge. Robinson states that "there is a prevailing perception that children should be sheltered from this knowledge for as long as possible in order to avoid any stress or trauma that might be associated with premature access to this information."[34] Here, difficult knowledge can be understood to be knowledge types that are similar to private and forbidden knowledge. Robinson argues that these attempts to shelter children from difficult knowledge, which is linked to powerful affective response in adults, are harmful as they deny children agency and the vocabulary to describe events in their own lives.[35]

Intellectual Freedom and Children

There are some who might argue that children and youth, who constitute the major locus of concern for the challengers in this study, should not have the same right to freely access information as adults. Although Robinson's work is primarily focusing on sexual knowledge, difficult knowledge can also include violence, racism, classism, and other harmful actions and structural inequities that have an impact on children's lives. As it is for adults, children and youth's right to intellectual freedom is a matter of social justice. As will be demonstrated in the analysis chapters, the arguments that challengers give regarding what is appropriate for children is often based on their own anxieties and concerns rather than those of children themselves. (In fact, as was the case in Westfield, New Jersey, youth often speak in support of the book challenge hearings.) It should also be noted that these arguments are used not only to shield children from certain types of knowledge but also to justify keeping certain types of knowledge from adults. For example, after *50 Shades of Grey* became a best seller, some public libraries refused to acquire it on the grounds that it is classified as erotica even though it is a novel intended for adults.[36] The definition of intellectual freedom given above helps us understand why it is imperative to understand the motivations and justifications of people who challenge books, as it is the cascading effects of censorship that matter most in an open society.

Censorship

Censorship, although related to intellectual freedom, is more difficult to define as the term itself is highly charged and political. *Merriam-Webster* defines censorship as "the institution system, or practice of censoring" or "the actions or practices of censors." The ALA defines censorship as "suppression of ideas and information that certain persons—individuals, groups or government officials—find objectionable or dangerous."[37] It is this definition that some both within and outside of librarianship find problematic. Is it possible for individuals to censor? Some argue that they cannot and that censorship is solely the purview of governments. James LaRue, a public library director, states that "censorship is the action by government officials to prohibit or suppress publications or services on the basis of their content."[38] As noted previously, this is in keeping with a narrow definition of censorship that focuses on government action rather than the actions of individuals or groups.[39] This study uses a more broad definition, and censorship is defined as any action that results in impeding a particular group of people's access to ideas or information. However, since the definition of censorship is both unsettled, and calling certain individuals or groups "censors" is highly political and somewhat pejorative, the term will not be used to describe the individuals in this study. Given this, those who request the removal or relocation of materials within library collections will be described as "challengers." The use of this term is described in more detail below.

Challenges

A challenge occurs when an individual or group asks library administration to remove, restrict, or relocate materials within libraries and schools. Challenges do not always lead to banning, that is, the removal of materials, or to a change in status such as restriction or relocation of the materials from library shelves. The cases generally follow a standard procedure in both libraries and schools: When an individual encounters objectionable material, that individual lodges a complaint with either the librarian or teacher (in schools sometimes the complaint goes to the principal). Challenges are often resolved at this point. If they are not, the challenger is given an opportunity to file an official complaint, usually in the form of a written request for reconsideration (see an example in appendix B). This is generally a standardized form used throughout the public institution's governance system. Following the filing of the request with the governing body, a series of meetings are held between administrators and challengers. If the matter is not resolved then, the challenge is escalated up the bureaucratic hierarchy, sometimes even concluding in a public hearing in front of the governing board for the institution. In other cases, governing bodies send the matter to a committee whose purpose is to discuss and determine the fate of the material.

The ALA's Office for Intellectual Freedom (OIF) tracks challenges to books throughout the country and makes the data publicly available on its website. Between 1990 and 2010, the OIF's statistics show that most challenges were initiated by parents and were for the following reasons (in descending order): sexuality, language, and "unsuited to" a particular age group (http://www.ala.org/advocacy/banned/frequentlychallenged/stats). The OIF, along with collecting statistics, also produces supporting material such as information on how to conduct a challenge hearing for libraries and librarians who are experiencing a challenge. In addition, the office provides institutional support for librarians who respond to challenges, including advice and monetary support if warranted.

Challengers

In this study, people who request the removal or relocation of materials within public institutions are called challengers. The ALA's statistics are somewhat vague in their characterization of challengers. The data set on the ALA's website titled "Challengers by Initiator" notes that challengers are administrators, board members, clergy, teachers, parents, pressure groups, and patrons. However, one might argue that the category "patron" overlaps significantly with the other categories. Although many challengers are individuals acting alone, there are some organizations, including Parents Against Bad Books in Schools (PABBIS) and Focus on the Family, that provide institutional support for challengers.[40] However, it seems that many challenges are sui generis. News accounts of challenges often share a general story line wherein a child brings a book home that his or her parent finds objectionable. The parent then files a complaint with the library or school. It is only after this complaint reaches the news media that the challengers are contacted by supporting organizations.

In this study, both the person who brings the original complaint and that person's supporters are called "challengers." They are constituted as an interpretive community that shares a particular symbolic universe and worldview—especially with regard to texts. First introduced by Stanley Fish in an essay written upon the publication of a new edition of Milton's poems, a community of interpreters is made up of those who share certain interpretive strategies for understanding texts. Fish argues that it is people's experiences that give text structure and that meaning is only created through interpretation. He specifically addresses literary critics by noting that they must also acknowledge that they are always interpreting and that they use specific strategies to do so. It is these interpretive strategies—which are shared by groups of people—that create the practice known as "reading" as well as the act of "writing." As Fish notes, "These strategies exist prior to the act of reading and therefore determine the shape of what is read rather than, as is usually assumed, the other way around."[41] This study attempts to delineate the interpretive strategies of challengers that shape how they read texts.

Worldview

Worldview is defined here as one's normal approach to understanding the world. It is both a road map for action and a framework for understanding everyday life events. The term is based on the work of Peter Berger and Thomas Luckmann, who define worldview as a "natural way of looking at the world."[42] Although it is possible that challengers do not share similar worldviews concerning other realms of life and experiences, as demonstrated in the analysis chapters, many of them have common views regarding their outlook on society, the role of public institutions in society, and the practice of reading implicit in the discourse of censorship.

THE CHALLENGE CASES

When originally designing the study, I intended to focus solely on challenges to materials in public and school libraries. However, as the research progressed, many challenges to materials in school curricula became part of the data set. The essential link between the schools and libraries is that they are both institutions within the public sphere and this status makes them targets of challengers. Challengers to books in curriculum also take the private act of choosing what their children will read by requesting an alternative for their own children and make it a public one by attempting to dictate what all other children will read. There is an a priori assumption that reading the book in question will be harmful to all children—not just their own. It is not surprising that parents have concerns about what their children will read, and the issue of required texts makes many parents uncomfortable. However, challengers' actions raise the question of why they are concerned about some books that are required reading and not others. One of the purposes of this study is to answer this question. In order to understand the relationship between power and knowledge it is necessary to analyze how people argue why certain texts should *not* be read, especially when they are required. Curriculum challenges are an important aspect of understanding these arguments since the element of coercion often amplifies the arguments regarding reading practices. It should also be noted that curriculum challenges often included requests to remove materials from both the school library and the classroom curriculum. As will be demonstrated in the analysis, challengers only differentiate between the two in order to bolster their specific challenge.

The final set for this study consisted of 15 challenge cases (see appendix C). The cases took place over a six-year period from 2007 to 2013, inclusive. Three of the cases—in Bedford, New Hampshire, Helena, Montana, and Westfield, New Jersey—were solely curriculum challenges. Nine cases were both curriculum and school library cases, and three were public library challenges. In order to be included in the study, a challenge case must have had the voice of a challenger in at least one of the data sources, which included transcripts of hearings, transcripts of interviews, and documents from the governing boards. More information regarding data gathering, analysis, and interpretation may be found in the Methodological Note (appendix A). Many of the original 25 cases were excluded for this reason. For example, the documents that were received through Freedom of Information Act (FOIA) requests might only include policy statements from the governing bodies.

The cases are described in more detail below and are listed in alphabetical order by location. Figure 1.1 is a map of the cases that shows that they took place in most regions of the United States with the exception of the Southwest. The majority of the cases were on the East Coast. Challenge cases are generally referenced by place throughout the analysis, as one of the primary features of the cases is that they involve the community and how it is viewed in the wider society. Throughout both the summaries below and the data analysis chapters that follow, challengers are also referenced by their location (e.g., the Central York challenger).

Bedford, New Hampshire (2011)

Bedford, New Hampshire, has experienced two recent challenge cases. The first, in 2010, concerned the book *Nickel and Dimed* by Barbara Ehrenreich. The data in this study focused on the second case regarding *Water for Elephants* by Sara Gruen, which a parent requested be removed from the local high school curriculum. I attended the public hearing for the book on February 28, 2011. The book was removed by the school district. Data for the case consisted of transcripts and fieldnotes from the hearing.

Carrollton, Texas (2011)

The challenge case in Carrollton, Texas, was unique in that it involved a child's caretaker instead of a parent. The challenger asked the Carrollton Public Library to remove *My Mom's Having a Baby* by Dori Hillestad Butler

Figure 1.1.   Map of challenge cases. *Map data © 2014 Google, INEGI*

from the children's collection after a child in her care checked it out. I interviewed the challenger in January of 2012. Along with a transcript of the interview, data from this case consisted of one request for reconsideration. The book was retained by the public library district.

Central York, Pennsylvania (2010)

In this case a parent challenged the inclusion of the book *Stolen Children* by Peg Kehret in the local elementary school library. Although I did receive a response to my request for documents from the Central York School District, it did not include any usable data. The book was retained by the school district. The challenger in the case sat for an interview with me in December of 2011, and a transcript of the interview is included in the data set.

Clarkstown, New York (2011)

Many school systems have lists of supplemental material for students to read, and a parent in Clarkstown, New York, challenged *The Perks of Being a Wallflower* by Stephen Chbosky for its inclusion on such a list. These cases lie in a grey area between curriculum and library challenges. The books are not required classroom texts, but they are recommended reading material and are therefore available in the school library. The book was retained on the list. Two requests for reconsideration constitute the data for this case.

Conway, South Carolina (2011)

Push by Sapphire was the target of a challenge in Conway, South Carolina, in 2011. According to records from the Horry County School Board, the book was inadvertently purchased for inclusion in classroom library shelves. That is, the book was intended for recreational student reading that could be obtained directly from the classroom and was not purchased for either the curriculum or the school library collection. A parent challenged the book when his or her child brought it home from school to read, and the book was ultimately removed from middle school library shelves. Due to a lack of information in news reports, it is unclear if the book remained in high school libraries. Data from the case consisted of hearing transcripts.

Greensboro, North Carolina (2010)

The Guilford County (North Carolina) Board of Education received a complaint regarding *Hoops* by Walter Dean Myers in December of 2010. The challenger requested that the book be removed from one of the local middle school's collections. Due to the lack of news reports and minutes from the board, the outcome of the case is unclear. Data from this case consisted of a request for reconsideration from the challenger.

Helena, Montana (2010)

A parent in Helena, Montana, challenged the inclusion of *The Absolutely True Diary of a Part-Time Indian* by Sherman Alexie in the local high school curriculum. A public hearing on the case was held on December 13, 2010. I interviewed the challenger one year later in December of 2012. The data for this case included a request for reconsideration, letters, transcripts of the public hearing, and the interview. The book was retained by the school system.

Lewiston, Maine (2007)

The challenge case in Lewiston, Maine, is somewhat notorious in library circles due to the fact that the case eventually entered the legal system. In August of 2007, a patron checked out the book *It's Perfectly Normal* by Robie H. Harris, a children's sexual education book, out of the local public library. Instead of returning it, she sent a letter with a check for the cost of the book to the library. The library refused to accept the check, and the patron was charged with civil theft. She pleaded not guilty and stood trial in front of a judge who ordered her to return the book. Eventually, the charges were dropped even though the book was not returned to the library. Data from this case included several letters and e-mails from the challenger.

Merrill, Wisconsin (2011)

The book *Montana 1948* by Larry Watson was the target of a curriculum challenge by 39 individuals in June of 2011. The book was retained by the school board. Although due to the similarity of the challengers' arguments it is likely that they worked as a group, there is no direct evidence of this as each of their challenges was presented to the school board individually. A hearing for the book was held on September 29, 2011. Data from the case consisted of all of the requests for recommendations, five letters, and transcripts of the hearing.

Randleman, North Carolina (2013)

This case is described more thoroughly in chapter 3. Briefly, a parent with a child in the Randolph County Public Schools challenged the book *Invisible Man* by Ralph Ellison. She asked that the book be removed from both the curriculum and school libraries. The book, though initially removed by the board, was eventually retained. Data for this case consisted of transcripts of hearings, interviews, and documents from the board.

Seattle, Washington (2010)

The challenge case in Seattle, Washington, received a fair amount of coverage in the media due to the classic status of the book in question, *Brave New World* by Aldous Huxley. The book was targeted for its inclusion in the local high school curriculum, and the school board eventually voted to retain it in the curriculum. However, the book was dropped from the required reading list of the originating school. Data for this case included letters and e-mails to the board.

Spring Hill, Florida (2010)

The seventh novel in the popular Alex Rider series, *Snakehead* by Anthony Horowitz, was challenged by a parent in Florida in October of 2010. The parent requested that the book be removed from all local elementary school libraries. Data from this challenge consisted of two requests for reconsideration. Both are by the same challenger and the latter is possibly due to the challenger's appeal of the initial governing body vote. The book was ultimately retained by the school district.

Stockton, Missouri (2010)

The Absolutely True Diary of a Part-Time Indian by Sherman Alexie was also the target of a challenge in Stockton, Missouri. The governing body treated the challenge as two separate challenges, one against inclusion in the curriculum and the other against inclusion in the school library. The board banned the book from the school curriculum and retained it in the library with circulation restrictions. A request for reconsideration, letters, and hearing transcripts constituted data for this challenge case.

West Bend, Wisconsin (2009)

The West Bend, Wisconsin, case also has some notoriety in the library world. Analysis of the case was one of the pilot cases for this study.[43] Briefly, the case began when the West Bend Public Library received a letter in its overnight drop box asking for links concerning LGBTQ youth to be removed from the library's website. Not long after, the library also received a letter from the same individuals requesting that several books on LGBTQ topics be removed from the young adult collection while others on "ex-gay therapy" be added to the collection. A public hearing for the case was held on June 2,

2009. The books were all retained. Data included letters, requests for recon-sideration, a petition, and hearing transcripts.

Westfield, New Jersey (2012)

The case in Westfield, New Jersey, described at the beginning of this chapter, centered on *The Absolutely True Diary of a Part-Time Indian*. The book, which was challenged for its inclusion in three freshman English classes in Westfield High School, was ultimately retained by the board, though parents may request a substitute. Data for this case includes transcripts of the hear-ing.

OUTLINE OF THE BOOK

The book begins with theory and then moves to analysis. Chapter 2 presents the theoretical frameworks employed in the study. First, it establishes the social constructionist metatheoretical orientation of the research. Second, it discusses the practice of reading, particularly as it relates to contemporary censorship, through a historical conceptual framework that emphasizes both physical practices and interpretive strategies that are applied to texts.

The third chapter is a case study of a challenge to *Invisible Man* by Ralph Ellison in Randleman, North Carolina, a town near Asheboro. Although the case lasted only two weeks, its political context and the swift reaction to the challenge offer a window into how book challenges operate in the United States and what they say about local communities, individual power, and the practice of reading.

Chapters 4 and 5 present the bulk of the analysis of the study. Chapter 4 focuses on challengers' construction of society, institutions, parenting, and childhood while chapter 5 discusses challengers' construction of the practice of reading. The final chapter discusses the language that challengers use and also analyzes some of the solutions that they propose.

NOTES

1. American Library Association, "Frequently Challenged Books of the 21st Century," n.d., http://www.ala.org/bbooks/frequentlychallengedbooks/top10.

2. Emily J. M. Knox, "The Books Will Still Be in the Library: Narrow Definitions of Censorship in the Discourse of Challengers," *Library Trends* 62, no. 4 (2014).

3. Sue Curry Jansen, *Censorship: The Knot That Binds Power and Knowledge* (New York: Oxford University Press, 1988).

4. Robert Darnton, *The Business of Enlightenment: A Publishing History of the 'Encyclop-édie,' 1775–1800* (Cambridge, MA: Belknap, 1979), 27.

5. Julian Petley, *Censorship: A Beginner's Guide* (Oxford: Oneworld, 2009).

6. Peter Burke, *A Social History of Knowledge: From Gutenberg to Diderot, Based on the First Series of Vonhoff Lectures Given at the University of Groningen (Netherlands)* (Malden, MA: Polity, 2000), 141.

7. For a detailed history of Anthony Comstock see Nicola Beisel, *Imperiled Innocents: Anthony Comstock and Family Reproduction in Victorian America* (Princeton, NJ: Princeton University Press, 1997).

8. Beisel, *Imperiled Innocents.*

9. Pierre Bourdieu, *Language and Symbolic Power* (Cambridge, MA: Harvard University Press, 1991).

10. Matthew Fishburn, *Burning Books* (New York, NY: Palgrave Macmillan, 2008); Rebecca Knuth, *Burning Books and Leveling Libraries: Extremist Violence and Cultural Destruction* (Westport, CT: Greenwood, 2006).

11. Reiner Keller, "Analysing Discourse: An Approach from the Sociology of Knowledge," *Forum Qualitative Sozialforschung/Forum: Qualitative Social Research* 6, no. 3 (2005), http://www.qualitative-research.net/index.php/fqs/article/view/19.

12. Keller, "Analysing Discourse," sec. 2.

13. Emily J. M. Knox, "Supporting Intellectual Freedom: Symbolic Capital and Practical Philosophy in Librarianship," *Library Quarterly* 84, no. 1 (2014): 1–14.

14. Robert P. Doyle, *Banned Books: Challenging Our Freedom to Read* (Chicago: American Library Association, 2010).

15. Alan Rubel, "Libraries, Electronic Resources, and Privacy: The Case for Positive Intellectual Freedom," *Library Quarterly* 84, no. 2 (April 2014): 183–208, doi:10.1086/675331.

16. American Library Association, *Intellectual Freedom Manual,* 8th ed. (Chicago: American Library Association, 2010); Barbara M. Jones and American Library Association Office for Intellectual Freedom, *Protecting Intellectual Freedom in Your Academic Library: Scenarios from the Front Lines* (Chicago: American Library Association, 2009); June Pinnell-Stephens and American Library Association Office for Intellectual Freedom, *Protecting Intellectual Freedom in Your Public Library: Scenarios from the Front Lines* (Chicago: American Library Association, 2012); Pat Scales and American Library Association Office for Intellectual Freedom, *Protecting Intellectual Freedom in Your School Library: Scenarios from the Front Lines* (Chicago: American Library Association, 2009).

17. Louise S. Robbins, *The Dismissal of Miss Ruth Brown: Civil Rights, Censorship, and the American Library* (Norman: University of Oklahoma Press, 2001); Shirley A. Wiegand and Wayne A. Wiegand, *Books on Trial: Red Scare in the Heartland* (Norman: University of Oklahoma Press, 2007).

18. Valerie Nye and Kathy Barco, *True Stories of Censorship Battles in America's Libraries* (Chicago: American Library Association, 2012).

19. Norman Poppel and Edwin M. Ashley, "Toward an Understanding of the Censor," *Library Journal* 111 (July 1986): 39–43.

20. James LaRue, *The New Inquisition: Understanding and Managing Intellectual Freedom Challenges* (Westport, CT: Libraries Unlimited, 2007), 51, 66.

21. Kelly Kingrey, "Perceptions of Intellectual Freedom among Conservative Christian Advocacy Groups: A Grounded Theory Analysis" (PhD diss., Texas Woman's University, 2005).

22. Loretta M. Gaffney, "Intellectual Freedom and the Politics of Reading: Libraries as Sites of Conservative Activism, 1990–2010" (PhD diss., University of Illinois at Urbana-Champaign, 2012).

23. An overview of research on intellectual freedom, primarily focused on challenges to children's literature, can be found in Christine A. Jenkins, "Book Challenges, Challenging Books, and Young Readers: The Research Picture," *Language Arts* 85, no. 3 (2008): 228.

24. Wayne A. Wiegand, "MisReading LIS Education," *Library Journal* 122, no. 11 (1997): 36–38.

25. Wayne A. Wiegand, "Tunnel Vision and Blind Spots: What the Past Tells Us about the Present; Reflections on the Twentieth-Century History of American Librarianship," *Library Quarterly* 69, no. 1 (1999): 1–32.

26. Sean Collins Walsh, "Seattle School Board Postpones Decision on Pulling 'Brave New World,'" *Seattle Times*, accessed July 16, 2014, http://seattletimes.com/html/localnews/2013460397_braveworld18m.html.

27. American Library Association, *Intellectual Freedom Manual*, xvii.

28. John Stuart Mill, *On Liberty* (Indianapolis: Hackett, 1978).

29. Article 18 states: "Everyone has the right to freedom of thought, conscience and religion; this right includes freedom to change his religion or belief, and freedom, either alone or in community with others and in public or private, to manifest his religion or belief in teaching, practice, worship and observance." Article 19: "Everyone has the right to freedom of opinion and expression; this right includes freedom to hold opinions without interference and to seek, receive and impart information and ideas through any media and regardless of frontiers." United Nations, The Universal Declaration of Human Rights, accessed July 16, 2014, http://www.un.org/en/documents/udhr/.

30. American Library Association, "Intellectual Freedom and Censorship Q & A," n.d., http://www.ala.org/Template.cfm?Section=basics&Template=/ContentManagement/ContentDisplay.cfm&ContentID=60610.

31. Eliza T. Dresang, "Intellectual Freedom and Libraries: Complexity and Change in the Twenty-First-Century Digital Environment," *Library Quarterly* 76, no. 2 (April 1, 2006): 169, doi:10.1086/506576.

32. Peter Johan Lor and Johannes Jacobus Britz, "Is a Knowledge Society Possible without Freedom of Access to Information?" *Journal of Information Science* 33, no. 4 (August 1, 2007): 387–97, doi:10.1177/0165551506075327.

33. Burke, *Social History of Knowledge*.

34. Kerry H. Robinson, *Innocence, Knowledge, and the Construction of Childhood: The Contradictory Nature of Sexuality and Censorship in Children's Contemporary Lives* (London: Routledge, 2013), 23.

35. Robinson, *Innocence, Knowledge*, 7, 23.

36. Bill Thompson, "County Library Shuns '50 Shades of Grey,'" *Ocala (FL) Star-Banner*, May 15, 2012, http://docs.newsbank.com.proxy2.library.illinois.edu/s/InfoWeb/aggdocs/AWNB/13ED04E00DD58100/0D0CB57DF8A1C275?s_lang.

37. American Library Association, "Intellectual Freedom and Censorship Q & A."

38. LaRue, *New Inquisition*, 3.

39. See Kingrey, "Perceptions of Intellectual Freedom."

40. Gaffney, "Intellectual Freedom."

41. Stanley Eugene Fish, *Is There a Text in This Class?* (Cambridge, MA: Harvard University Press, 1982), 171.

42. Peter L. Berger and Thomas Luckmann, *The Social Construction of Reality* (New York: Anchor, 1966), 8.

43. Emily J. M. Knox, "The Challengers of West Bend: The Library as a Community Institution," in *Libraries and the Reading Public in Twentieth-Century America*, ed. Christine Pawley and Louise S. Robbins (Madison: University of Wisconsin Press, 2013), 200–16.

Chapter Two

Power and Knowledge

Most of my interviews take place over the phone. This is not ideal, as quite a bit of the interaction is lost when you can't see someone's nonverbal communication. Despite these drawbacks, my recorder is on and I'm concentrating on being an active listener. The interview begins with questions about the participant's life and how reading fits into it and only later on do we discuss the book challenge. The reasons for the book challenge in this particular case are notable. In the United States many books are challenged for their sexual or political content, but this parent was concerned about the violence in the text. I ask her about her reasons for challenging the book:

> I think it's damaging for children to read literature, damages them psychologically . . . that literature, not dark as in Harry Potter dark. But dark as in holding a gun to the head and describing holding a knife to a two-year-old's throat. That's just too graphic. Too much. Crossing a line. If they weren't doing a story about a kidnapping they wouldn't have . . . you know they get kidnapped and trapped in a closet. But it [should] never [cross] that line where somebody is holding a knife to her throat. To me the line has been crossed and I felt like I had to stand up and say my piece about it. (Interview with challenger, Central York, PA, December 7, 2011)

Although the stated reasons for targeting this particular book are not typical, the parent's justifications for wanting the book removed can be found in many challenge cases: "A line has been crossed." "I needed to say something." "The books will damage children." These themes occur with regularity in challengers' arguments for removing a particular title from a public library or school. As noted in chapter 1, censorship demonstrates an intimate relationship between power and knowledge. When a group or individual endeavors to remove, restrict, or relocate an item within a public institution they are both demonstrating their concern over the knowledge contained within the book and also exercising their symbolic power over the institution. This chapter explores these concepts more fully, first by introducing a theory of power—specifically, symbolic power—and second by exploring the construction of knowledge and the practice of reading.

By way of introduction to these theoretical frameworks, note that this study is a work of discourse analysis. There are many different types of discourse analysis (see the Methodological Note in appendix A for more on this method of analysis). According to Nelson Phillips and Cynthia Hardy, discourse is "an interrelated set of texts and practices of their production, dissemination, and reception that brings an object into being."[1] More specifically, discourse is constructed from language. However, it is not simply "words" that exist outside of a particular individual but also what individuals "do" with the language. The theories given below describe how language is "constitutive of reality."[2] Language does not simply describe the world—it also constructs the objects that exist within it. The challengers' arguments analyzed in the following chapters use language that both describes and constructs their worldviews concerning society, the materiality of books, the act of reading, and institutions within their communities.

The chapter begins with a discussion of social constructionism, the meta-theoretical framework for the study that clarifies the emphasis on language in the analysis. It then discusses symbolic capital and power in the theory of Pierre Bourdieu as these two ideas help to explain the intersection of language and power that are employed in challenge cases. These two theories clarify the emphasis on language in the analysis. Next, the chapter explores how past and present reading practices can be used to understand the current reading practices of challengers. Although these frameworks for analysis come from different paradigms, they provide robust concepts and vocabulary for understanding the discourse of challengers and also position their discourse within a broader social-theoretical framework.

SOCIAL CONSTRUCTIONISM AND SYMBOLIC POWER

The analysis in this study is based in the work of Peter Berger and Thomas Luckmann's *The Social Construction of Reality*.[3] In this classic treatise in the sociology of knowledge, Berger and Luckmann explore how reality is constructed through everyday knowledge that is transmitted and maintained through society and its institutions. The book describes how "language marks the co-ordinates of [one's] life in society and fills that life with meaningful objects."[4] Based on the work of Max Scheler, Robert Merton, Karl Mannheim, and others, Berger and Luckmann posit two concepts from their work that are particularly important for the analysis used in this study: stocks of knowledge and the symbolic universe.

Stocks of Knowledge

In order to understand what Berger and Luckmann mean by "stocks of knowledge" it is necessary to understand their theory of how language and the social world operate as the foundation of reality in everyday life. Language, including written language, is used for the *objectivation* of things as well as a bridge to experience and organize everyday life. Note that the term "objects" is used broadly in this context and includes both everyday objects such as books as well as institutions such as the school or library. Through the process of objectivation we develop a system of signs through which we build up a socially distributed stock of knowledge. Stocks of knowledge are based in language and include both everyday and specialized knowledge. Everyday knowledge includes, for example, the ability to read and write. Specialized knowledge, on the other hand, is the domain of experts within a particular field. This would include, for example, the knowledge that subject librarians have for sources in a particular area of study or the knowledge of programmers of coding languages.

Prior to publishing *The Social Construction of Reality*, Luckmann coauthored *The Structure of the Life-World* with Alfred Schutz, in which the concept of stocks of knowledge is described in more detail.[5] Here Luckmann and Schutz demonstrate how stocks of knowledge are constituted by both *types* and *typical actions*. Types are individuals' construction of objects in their everyday life—including their fellow human beings—that are developed through a process of socialization. Schutz and Luckmann note that these types are abstract, incomplete, relative, and relevant to the situation at hand. That is, they do not provide a "complete picture" but are used as a heuristic device to interpret situations and objects in one's life. Types also are mutable depending on the intimacy and relevance of the involved object. For example, a book is a type of object for which I might have a general perception in my head, but this perception will change when I encounter a book in my everyday life. I will also employ my construction of "book" to perceive and identify that the object in front of me is, in fact, a book. However, depending on the nature of the interaction, this encounter might also change my typification of books in general. It is salient for this study to note that types can also apply to institutions such as the library or schools. An individual's particular understanding of "what a library should do" or "what a school should be" within a community is based on a typification of "library" and "school." As will be demonstrated in the following chapters, challengers argue that such institutions should be "safe"—not just physically but also in terms of having "appropriate" types of knowledge on shelves or in curricula. A typical action describes how one responds to others' actions and provides information on how to get things accomplished. One example of typical actions that is salient to this study is the interpretive strategies that one uses when reading a text. For example, when the interviewee quoted above states that reading "dark" literature damages children psychologically, she is describing a particular interpretation that she brings to the text. According to Berger and Luckmann, stocks of knowledge are learned through socialization. Types and typical actions are passed down from one generation to the next through social institutions such as the family and schools. Stocks of knowledge operate within what Berger and Luckmann call the symbolic universe, which both produces new interpretations of objects and makes these interpretations credible.

The Symbolic Universe

The symbolic universe, as described by Berger and Luckmann, is particularly important to understanding the worldviews and arguments of challengers, as it is a concept that helps to illuminate the origin of the common themes found in their discourse. Objective reality, that is, the reality of everyday life, is constructed through processes of institutionalization and legitimation. Types and typical actions that make up stocks of knowledge are passed down through these two processes. Institutionalization describes the process of socialization that takes place through childhood. Individuals become "selves" through a process of social integration with both their environment and other humans. One's "self" is the outcome of all of these interactions. Legitimation, on the other hand, is the process by which institutionalization is made plausible and passed from one generation to the next. The symbolic universe, through which meaning is created, emerges from this process of legitimation as it makes stocks of knowledge credible to succeeding generations. The symbolic universe encompasses all levels of legitimation in everyday life including the incipient or "things are just like that" level, theoretical propositions, and explicit theories. These legitimating functions allow the symbolic universe to play an important part in constructing an individual's worldview because it supplies meaning to unexplained and random events and helps to explain divergent worldviews among individuals.

Symbolic universes perform important functions within objective reality. First, they have a "law-giving" quality and allow for everyday life to have complete integration. They also order one's individual biography and provide legitimacy for death. In short, symbolic universes provide a basis for rationalizing the events in one's life and are an integral part of one's worldview. For example, religion operates as a symbolic universe sine qua non since it completely orders reality. As noted above, symbolic universes provide a foundation for an institutional order for the entire universe and help individuals fill in gaps for aspects of life that are not readily explained. As will be demonstrated in chapter 6, some challengers sometimes use religious language to argue for removing or relocating a particular text. It is clear from this use of language that, for these challengers, their religious beliefs provide a particular order for understanding their lives.

Social constructionism, as briefly outlined above, provides the metatheoretical foundation for this study because it offers a framework for understanding how language shapes an individual's worldview on the deepest levels of legitimation and rationalization. For Berger, Luckmann, and Schutz, the constitutive view of language is axiomatic. Since this is a study of the discourse employed by individuals in challenge cases, it is important to understand how analysis of language provides a window into the wider worldviews of challengers. That is, it is possible to understand why challengers target particular books in an age of ubiquitous access to texts by exploring the language they employ to justify their actions. As noted previously, this study can be classified as culturalist discourse research that explores the arguments challengers use to justify their arguments for removing, relocating, or restricting books in public school libraries. Research of this type focuses on how both language and symbolic capital affect the distribution of knowledge. While the previous section of this chapter discussed language, the following section explores Pierre Bourdieu's theory of practice and symbolic power.

Symbolic Capital and Power

As will be demonstrated in the analysis chapters, challengers use their symbolic power as citizens, parents, and taxpayers in challenge cases in order to shape public institutions in their communities. The symbolic is an important aspect of Bourdieu's philosophical project, the development of a theory of practice. Bourdieu's project is called theory of *practice* because it focuses on how individuals conduct themselves within both institutional and personal constraints.[6] According to Bourdieu, constructions within the social world have three attributes: First, they are always subject to structure. Second, cognition is socially structured. Finally, practices are both individual and social. Bourdieu's well-known concept of *habitus* comes out of these three points—it is what produces structure for classification within the world. The concept of habitus is crucial to understanding Bourdieu's theory.[7] It describes how individuals operate within the "space" between objective structures and subjective structures. As Bourdieu notes, practice is never automatic and people do not always know that they are operating within socially constructed boundaries. By turning "history into nature" and "nature into common sense," an individual's habitus offers a collection of repertoires on which an individual can draw throughout a particular event.[8] In this study, one set of repertoires on which challengers rely are particular reading strategies that are based on a strong correlation between the written word and the idea of truth. In Bourdieu's terms, challengers' habitus provides the structures for interpreting text in this manner. It is important to note that the world is not seen by people as being completely structured—individuals have "space" in which to operate and interact within the symbolic system.

Another important aspect of Bourdieu's theory is the concept of capital. Capital refers to an individual's "accumulated labor which, when appropriated on a private, i.e., exclusive basis by agents or groups of agents, enables them to appropriate social energy in the form of reified or living labor."[9] In other words, capital is a form of currency broadly construed. According to Bourdieu, there are four different types of capital that an individual possesses: economic, cultural, social, and symbolic. First, economic capital is simply one's monetary worth. Next, Bourdieu describes three different states of cultural capital. Art, music, and literature are examples of cultural capital in its objectified state. Second, table manners and other such habits of the body exemplify an embodied state of cultural capital. Finally, academic credentials are an institutionalized form of cultural capital. The third type of capital, social capital, is particularly important for this study because it primarily consists of one's social networks which can be leveraged for political influence in the local community. Social capital also includes one's inherited capital such as is found in the nobility.

Symbolic capital is a "transformed and thereby disguised form of physical 'economic' capital that produces its proper effect inasmuch and only inasmuch, as it conceals the fact that it originates in 'material' forms of capital which are also, in the last analysis, the source of its effects."[10] That is, symbolic capital is economic capital in a different form. For example, when challengers describe themselves as "taxpayers" they are conveying the idea that they have a certain kind of fiscal authority over public institutions. This is a method of converting one's economic capital into power. Symbolic power is important because it is often misrecognized as something else such as common sense or justified actions. Bourdieu defines symbolic power as those symbolic instruments (including discourse) that are used by one social group to dominate another social group.[11] Both the division of labor and ideology are included as types of symbolic power, and it is understood to be one of the primary building blocks for a social group.

It is the combination of symbolic capital and symbolic power that delineates the knowledge classification struggles found in challenge cases. These cases are a struggle for domination over who has the authority to determine the boundaries of legitimate and illegitimate knowledge in the public sphere. Challengers use their own symbolic power against the symbolic power of librarians, teachers, and administrators. Bourdieu describes this struggle as a form of symbolic violence in which hegemonic norms and procedures are used by one group to dominate over another.[12] As will be demonstrated in the following chapters, challenge cases are essentially symbolic struggles between individuals and groups who have different values and operate within differing symbolic universes. The following section discusses the foundations of one aspect of the symbolic universe in which challengers operate—their conceptualization of the book and the interpretive strategies that they impose on texts.

WRITTEN KNOWLEDGE

In his book on understanding and managing challenges titled *The New Inquisition*, James LaRue, a former public library director, argues that book challenges are essentially about respect for writing:

> Behind the challenges of many patrons is awe of the written word. This may well be rooted in the profound respect granted to the Bible, based on several factors but not least upon its endurance. This belief, incidentally, is also shared by the secular left, which believes education—mainly exposure to the written word—is also very powerful.[13]

That is, understanding an individual's reverence for the written word is foundational for understanding why he or she challenges a book. This argument can be found throughout challengers' discourse. Within this particular worldview, it is easy to see why challengers are arguing that children should not read a particular book because reading is a powerful act—one that has effects on individual character and behavior. While the sections above focused on theories of discourse and power, the following sections elucidate the other half of the censorship equation—a particular understanding of knowledge and how it operates in everyday life.

Grounded in the idea of the power of writing, the following explores how past and present reading practices can be used to understand challengers' construction of current interpretive strategies. Since the practices of writing and reading have changed over time, it is necessary to define what these practices are and how they may influence contemporary challengers. This section begins with a discussion of writing practices and the materiality of books. It then offers a brief overview of historical reading practices in the West, starting in the Middle Ages through to the contemporary era. Finally, this overview offers a framework for understanding how the "undisciplined imagination" is conceptualized in challengers' discourse.

Writing Practices

Writing, in contrast to oration, is a form of symbolic authority that acquires its power through material form. Writing is a performative action and its real-world effects outstrip the physical action of putting words to page.[14] There are many examples of this performative power of writing. Some legal contracts, for example, are not considered binding unless they are written down. This can be most clearly seen in the common legal agreement of marriage. Even if there is a ceremony, there is no marriage without a written and signed marriage license. Another example concerns the institution of slavery. Before manumission, the act of writing someone's name under the heading "slave" made them a slave.[15] When the slave's owner struck through his or name on this list, the slave was free. However, freedmen and freed-women were required to carry papers that proved their status in society. These acts of writing had and have actual ramifications in the "real world."

It is a complex task to conceptualize how writing produces these effects. In the Western world the writing practices described above seem to operate as indexical signs. A concept first developed by Charles S. Peirce, an indexical sign has a tangible link between the signifier and the signified where there is a *correlation* between the meaning of the sign and reality.[16] In this case, there is a correlation between writing and reality. Indexical signs indicate a concrete reality: It is a sign wherein "smoke means fire, pawprints mean the presence of a cat."[17] In the example given above, the words on the page (e.g., a person's name under the heading "slave") have a direct correlation with his or her status in the reality. Further, the writing imbues the individual with that status. Another example of the indexical status of writing might be the words on a legal contract, or the act of signing a marriage license signifying an ontological change among the signatories. At the same time, it also produces this change. That is, by signing the marriage license the two individuals are now "married" and they are now bound to fulfill the duties that go along with that status. Note that these writing practices take place within wider institutional and social contexts that continually construct the written word as a powerful act. As demonstrated in this study, challengers are very concerned with truth in the written word and it is possible that this is due to understanding of text in this sense where the text operates as an indexical sign. That is, the fact that something is written text means that is (or should be) true. This concept of correlation between the sign of the text and signified reality is particularly helpful in understanding challengers' discourse regarding the nature of truth and fictional texts as described in chapter 5.

Writing, which in its performative capacity can give shape and framework to the social world, also has a direct influence on the authority given to books in modern society. Because they "contain" writing and are a fixed medium, books also have a particular kind of "power." They operate as symbolic, stabilizing objects within the social world that can legitimate the ideas that are contained within them. That is, the book *as a book* legitimizes and gives credibility to ideas in texts. This connection between writing and books is a major theme in the discourse of censorship. One model for understanding this relationship between texts and books can be found in the work of Lisa Jardine, who titles one chapter in her monograph "The Triumph of the Book." Jardine notes that books "revolutionized the transmission of knowledge and permanently changed the attitudes of thinking Europe."[18] It is the book as a medium for the dissemination of knowledge that is crucial here, as its material form allowed for the spread of a limitless number of ideas across the West and throughout the world. As demonstrated in the analysis chapters that follow, challengers are finely attuned to the legitimating power of writing and its influence over people in the sense that this power can validate the assumption presented in a particular text.

Materiality of Books

If one allows that, for challengers, the book is a symbolic object of authority, it must be noted that this authority is complicated by the fact that books may contain limitless content and ideas. As a consequence of this, books are simultaneously a stabilizing and a destabilizing force in society. A common theme in challengers' discourse centers on whether or not the presence of a controversial idea in a book gives legitimacy to the idea as such. Their arguments reveal the tension between the book as a stabilizing and destabilizing object. Book history scholarship demonstrates that the book operates not only as a legitimizing agent but also as a symbolic object that can be used to verify one's particular cultural sensibility. For example, during the early modern period, simply having a copy of the *Encyclopédie* on one's library shelf demonstrated a particular sensibility and showed that the owner shared the progressive opinions of the *philosophes* who wrote the articles in the encyclopedia.[19] Another historical example that demonstrates the importance of the book's symbolic authority is the reverence that the 19th-century New England families described by William J. Gilmore held for their single-volume Bibles. Even if the household had no other books, there was always a Bible, which served as a family archive and a manual for living.[20] This concept of the book as signifier of one's sensibilities is linked to challengers' concern over having objectionable material in public institutions such as libraries and schools. If such books are present it means that, for the challengers, the institutions approve of all aspects of the texts within. In her monograph on a censorship controversy in Oklahoma, Louise Robbins argues that libraries are particularly susceptible to challenges and that this "vulnerability comes both from the importance and authority Americans accord the books . . . the library collects, organizes and circulates . . . from its position as a public institution charged with the preservation and transmission of culture."[21] For challengers, having a book in a public or school library collection, and especially if the book is approved for use in a school curriculum, means that the institution believes in the ideas that are presented in the text. In this context, ownership of books becomes a sign of a particular worldview.

It should be noted that perhaps the most well-known debate in the area of the authority of the book relates to the relationship between the presentation of the text and how it is interpreted by readers. In her treatise on the impact of printing on Western society, Elizabeth Eisenstein argues that printing changed culture not simply because ideas shifted but because the printing press allowed many more people to have access to these new ideas.[22] Eisenstein contends that printing allowed for the standardization of texts (i.e., fixity) and permitted people to discuss the same work across space and time. There are some historians who consider Eisenstein's argument to be overly deterministic. Adrian Johns, in particular, believes the idea of fixity in early printing to be overstated.[23] He argues that early modern printings of books were not uniform editions of texts and therefore could not be considered to be a source of stable knowledge. Nevertheless, the idea of the fixed work underpins and enables the practice of indexing the book and allows for ideas to be maintained over temporal and spatial distances. Challengers, like almost all contemporary readers, take this idea of fixity of the text as a given and assume that the text they are challenging is the same for all.

The juxtaposition of the book as a revered material object and the importance of the text contained therein is also emphasized by Daniel Selcer in his monograph on early modern philosophy titled *Philosophy and the Book*. Of particular interest is Selcer's discussion of Baruch Spinoza and how the mechanized printed word changed people's interpretation of text especially in relation to the Bible. Selcer notes that Spinoza posits two somewhat contradictory positions. First, that scripture itself is a fixed entity but its new status as simply "a book" means that it has lost some of its sacred character. Second and concurrently, that sacred meaning is inextricable from the materiality of the text.[24] The words on the page are capable of creating real effects on the reader:

> A concatenation of letters on the page is capable of generating in me devotion to God (or its opposite . . .) means the disposition of these letters produces effects in my mind and in my body, and that those effects are transitions in my power to produce effects (i.e., to act and to exist). This is what constitutes the meaning of the words in question: the meaning of words is nothing but the effects they produce.[25]

This idea of meaning and interpretation, even in the secular realm, leading to real effects is integral to understanding the discourse of censorship as a whole and discourse of challengers in particular. As demonstrated in the analysis chapters, challengers often fear that reading the targeted texts will not only lead to short-term harmful effects but also puts the reader's soul in jeopardy. The book, as a material object that both stabilizes and transmits knowledge, is of primary importance to understanding how these effects become manifest in a reader. The circular interaction between books and texts means that these material objects have the power to affect an individual's character and soul. The next section of this chapter describes in more detail some models for understanding how this takes place by exploring the historical models that inform challengers' construction of the practice of reading, in particular with regard to the effects of texts on certain readers.

HISTORICAL READING PRACTICES

Reading, like writing, is somewhat difficult to theorize. In this study, reading is constructed as a social practice that has changed over time and encompasses different physical modalities and interpretive strategies. In order to understand why people challenge books, it is necessary to delve into their understanding of how reading works, what it means to read a text, and how they construct the idea of "appropriate" reading materials. In her article on textual interpretation, Elizabeth Long demonstrates the social and collective nature of the practice of reading.[26] Even though reading is often seen as a solitary activity (a concept that Long vividly illustrates through a series of images that show lone readers), Long establishes the collective nature of reading by demonstrating its reliance on both social infrastructure and social framing. By social infrastructure, Long means that reading is an activity that is learned through social relationships and relies on the social base of literary culture. Social framing constructs certain materials as being "worth reading" and is a socially defined concept. As shown in the following chapters, this concept of "worthy" reading becomes visible in challengers' discourse when they refer to the challenged material as "garbage" or "junk" in opposition to books that they consider to be worth reading.

The following sections of the chapter briefly describe reading practices from the Middle Ages to the present with particular emphasis on the interpretive strategies employed when encountering written texts.[27] Here one can see the development of "typical actions" with regard to reading. Stanley Fish notes that "interpretive strategies are not put into execution after reading . . . they are the shape of reading and because they are the shape of reading they give texts their shape, making them rather than, as it is usually assumed, arising from them."[28] As Fish explains, the meaning of a text is never fixed and is open to polysemy (i.e., multiple meanings) across time, groups of people, or even within a single individual. Interpretive strategies are defined here as a set of implicit decisions regarding analysis that one makes both before and while one is reading. These decisions have many different influences including how written texts are socially constructed and, as noted previously, the perceived authority of the book. As will be shown in the analysis chapters, challengers, in fact, disagree with this view of texts being open to many different meanings and often argue that there is only one possible interpretation of the texts that they target.

The Middle Ages

Historians have shown that in the Middle Ages, writing was understood to be a medium of authority that held the record of obligations of the poor and had both magic and evil powers.[29] This conceptualization can be connected to the performative aspects of writing described above. It was, according to historical accounts, an era of "restricted literacy" in which few people could read or write. Restricted literacy is defined as a society in which only the gentry, clerics, and other elites are able to read—everyone else lives on the margins of these literate classes.[30] This meant, ipso facto, that problematic texts were not accessible to most of the population. Many people could not read and those who could did so primarily for religious purposes. Christianity is a religion whose doctrines are based almost exclusively on texts. The Christian canon consists of the written texts of the Hebrew Bible (or Old Testament—one section of which is called "The Writings") and the New Testament that includes the four canonical written Gospels and letters to Christian communities from wandering apostles. For the Christian, almost everything that one needed to know for salvation was contained in these texts and he or she considered reading to be the path to redemption. As will be demonstrated in the analysis chapters, the negative of this idea (that reading can be a pathway to sin) is a common theme in challengers' discourse.

Levels of Interpretation

In the Middle Ages, those who could read would often engage with scripture—and possibly other texts—on a dialogical level. They would employ interpretive strategies that did not encourage a single fixed meaning but, as described below, methods that allowed for simultaneous polysemy of a given text. These codified interpretive strategies were intended to guide the reader away from a negative interpretive pathway of sin. According to M. B. Parkes, there were four levels of interpretation that readers used when studying texts. The first was *lectio*, in which the student had to identify the elements of the text. *Emendatio* referred to the corrections made by the student to the manuscript text. The third, *enarratio*, described the process of interpreting the text's subject matter. Finally, *iudicium* referred to judgment of the aesthetic qualities of the text. Discrepancies in texts, especially sacred texts, could be attributed to the multiple senses of scripture.[31] Scholars engaged with and produced their own personal readings or exegesis of texts through a process that was fully systematized. Although, as time went on, students used a variety of glosses and abridgments to help them better understand difficult texts, all were encouraged to be readers and not simply reciters. For example, Jacqueline Hamesse offers an anecdote of Robert of Melun who, next to a passage on *lectors* and *recitators* writes: "Concerning those who apply themselves to the exercises of reading and citations of authorities and do not understand them."[32] In this time period, there were professional recitators who simply read aloud while lectors were those who attempted to read and understand the text.

Silent Reading and Private Interpretation

According to accounts of the history of reading, physical reading practices shifted during the Middle Ages. Hamesse discusses modes of reading that existed at the time. First, people read by murmuring in low voices to themselves. People also continued to read aloud publicly—a practice that dated from antiquity.[33] Third, although it took some time for this practice to take hold, Hamesse notes that people also read silently. When reading silently—in contrast to reading aloud—one's thoughts and therefore one's interaction with the text is private. This historical shift to silent reading is important for understanding the discourse of challengers. When someone reads silently, an observer has no knowledge of how the reader is interpreting the text. Paul Saenger notes that the connection between silent reading and accusations of heresy began in the 11th century. Reading aloud in community (public *lectio*) meant that others would be able to provide corrections to heretical statements. Saenger explicitly links the spread heresy to the silent, private reading of tracts:

> Alone in his study, the author, whether a well-known professor or an obscure student, could compose or read heterodox ideas without being overheard. In the classroom, the student, reading silently to himself, could listen to the orthodox opinions of his professor and visually compare them with the views of those who rejected established ecclesiastical authority. . . . Private visual reading and composition thus encouraged individual critical thinking and contributed ultimately to the development of skepticism and intellectual heresy.[34]

When one reads silently, one could be thinking heretical thoughts and there is no method for correcting them. This point of distinction between reading silently and reading aloud is vitally important for understanding the discourse of contemporary challengers. Silent reading places interpretation primarily in the hands of the individual. As demonstrated in the following chapters, the issue of unmediated text is a salient one for understanding the actions of challengers. While other mediums, such as broadcast television, can be censored by standards and practices boards, reading silently means that outsiders do not know where one is located or how one might be interpreting the text. This adds to the fear challengers have that people will have access to the ideas presented in objectionable texts.

Early Modern Period (1500–1800)

Along with changes to reading practices in the Middle Ages described above, new reading practices in the early modern period also provide models for understanding some distinctive aspects of challengers' construction of reading in the early 21st century. Several shifts in reading practices described by historians in this period appear in the discourse of contemporary challengers. Some notable differences in the practice of reading include an emphasis on unmediated texts and the fear of the effects of unmediated interpretation; along with these practices there was also increased distributions of printed materials and a continuing growth of literacy throughout the time period. Each of these changes is briefly described below.

Unmediated Texts

As noted above, silent reading became a more widespread practice during the Middle Ages. Without the intervention of fellow "readers" who were listening to a text as it was read out loud, reading became a personal, individualized experience between the reader and the text. The text itself, however, often had its own mediatory attributes. As Brian Stock notes, there were "textual communities" or "'microsocieties' that shared a common understanding of scripture."[35] Sacred and classical works usually included annotations, glosses, and commentaries that would guide the reader toward a "correct" interpretation of the original text. According to Stock, individuals who shared a particular understanding of the text became a community even if they were dissimilar in other ways.

During the early modern period, sacred and classical works that were published in their original languages circulated without commentaries and annotations.[36] This particular model of reading did not focus on the interpretations of others; instead, historians argue that individuals could form interpretations of classics unmediated by the annotations of other readings. Similar to the Middle Ages, when a "typical" reader who read silently no longer had to contend with the influence of others who were *hearing* the same text, during the early modern age, the "typical" reader did not always have to contend with the work of others in the text itself. As a consequence of this, interpretive strategies that one brought to the text exerted considerable influence when reading a text. It should be noted that humanist scholars in the early modern age eventually produced their own commentaries and these were often published alongside the original text. As Anthony Grafton writes, "The glosses of humanist teacher, usually offered first as lessons in classrooms, then rewritten for print, twined themselves like the illuminators' vines around the texts."[37] However, the early modern age also placed considerable emphasis on the individual and his own interpretation of the texts. As described by Grafton, often readers would write their own annotations to supplement the printed ones, thus revealing their individual interpretation of the texts.

The early modern age was also a time of religious upheaval in Europe. Although there were many doctrinal variations in what eventually became Protestant Christianity, one—*sola scriptura* or salvation through knowledge of the Bible alone—is particularly important for understanding the contemporary discourse of challengers as it points to why reading is such a powerful activity. Inherent in this idea is the belief that each person can read and understand for himself or herself the truth of the good news of Jesus Christ.[38] Along with the doctrine of the priesthood of all believers (a belief that there is no mediator between the believer and God), the doctrine of *sola scriptura* indicates a belief that each person can bring about his or her own salvation through reading. These shifts, along with the loss of the fourfold sense of scripture described above, are crucial for understanding how contemporary challengers construct the practice of reading.

The Consequences of Unmediated Interpretation

When one considers the doctrine of *sola scriptura*, it is not surprising, then, that Protestant reformers viewed the practice of reading with some trepidation. This doctrine as well as the practice of reading unmediated texts silently led to two contradictory notions regarding reading the Bible. First, since the reformers assumed that God wants to save his people, the Bible was considered to be a simple text for anyone to understand. However, reformers simultaneously feared that this might not be the case and were concerned that individual interpretations might lead to heresy—the negative interpretation described above.[39] This fear was, in some respects, exacerbated by the events of the Peasants' War (1524–1525) in which tenant farmers animated by the antiauthoritarian doctrines of the revolution rose up against feudal lords. Martin Luther, in particular, was highly influenced by the war and published commentaries and catechisms on the scriptures in order to guide his followers toward "correct" interpretation.[40]

As noted earlier, fear of unmediated interpretation is critical for understanding the discourse of contemporary challengers. As Martyn Lyons notes:

> Neither Protestant writers nor the Catholic hierarchy could predict readers'
> responses. Lutherans, Calvinists and Inquisitors alike confronted the indepen-
> dence of individual readers who could not easily be influenced or guided in the
> desired direction. . . . The interpretation of scripture could not be controlled.[41]

In the early modern age, reformers encouraged their followers to read on
their own but with a reference text to guide them. These readers were not
"trusted" to arrive at this correct interpretation on their own. This is an
argument similar to those made by challengers. Although the segments of
society who are not trusted to have adequate interpretive skills have changed
over time, this study demonstrates that the fear of unmediated interpretation
is paramount to understanding why people challenge materials in public
institutions.

Increased Distribution and Literacy

Along with an increase in unmediated texts and the fear of how individuals
would interpret such texts, the early modern period also saw the advent of the
printing press and greater distribution of texts as well as increased literacy.
As noted earlier, Jardine argues that the book altered the nature of knowledge
in Western society.[42] How this happened and the nuances of this change
remain highly contested among scholars. One of Jardine's explanations for
this change, that books were less expensive than manuscripts, seems the most
salient for understanding of the discourse of censorship. Since books were
less expensive they were (eventually) more widely disseminated in society.
This meant that more people might have access to knowledge that was not
previously readily available to them. And yet by implication, people were in
danger of becoming poor interpreters of texts.

According to some accounts of history, not only were there more texts
available for reading in the early modern period, there were also more people
to read them. The spread of literacy during this time period is well documented.[43] For the purposes of this study, it is important to note that this
increase in the literate populace meant that more people would be susceptible
to the dangers of the unmediated text. One might surmise that as more people
were able to engage in the practice of reading, anxieties that they would do so
"incorrectly" would also be intensified. This fear of unmediated interpretation relates to the concept of "undisciplined imagination" described in more
detail below and helps inform some of the unease found in challengers'
discourse on reading.

Modern Period (1800–Present)

During the 19th century, some sources note that there was a "print explosion"
in the modern world.[44] Technological changes eventually gave rise to the

mass production of books, which meant that many different types of texts were available to many different members of society. Books were no longer the province of the wealthy. A few notable changes in reading took place during this time period. Both Europe and the United States experienced a reading fever, characterized by marked rises in literacy and the "secularization" of literature. Particularly important to understanding the discourse of censorship are the concepts of critical distance to the text and commonsense interpretive strategies. These latter changes are described in some depth below.

Secularization and Extensive Reading

According to William J. Gilmore, the secularization of reading material occurred more slowly in the United States than in Europe. Even if the household had no other books, there was always a Bible present in the homes of the New England families. For 19th-century American families, the family Bible served as both a family archive and a manual for living.[45] However, reading fever for texts other than the Bible grew in the antebellum period, and the reading public in the United States became especially enamored of novels, which "threatened not just to coexist with elite literature but to replace it."[46] There was a fear of a reading public who subsisted on popular literature that is familiar to many observers in contemporary America.

Individuals also began to read texts less intensively. Rolf Engelsing's well-known theory regarding intensive versus extensive reading primarily refers to practices of the bourgeois in 18th-century Germany; however, because of the slower pace of change in reading practices in the United States, his thesis regarding changes in reading practices provides a useful starting point for understanding the practice of reading in the modern age in America.[47] Intensive reading, a style that characterized many readers up to this point, involved reading a few items closely, while extensive reading describes reading many items with less care. Leah Price argues that Engelsing established a contrast between "reverent readers and passive consumers . . . [that] fuels a conservative distaste for modern mass culture and mass markets."[48] This distaste for mass culture and mass reading was marked in this time of reading fever and is well documented in Stephen Colclough's *Consuming Texts*, which uses newspaper illustrations from the industrial age to demonstrate this leeriness toward the reading public. One such illustration shows a father ignoring his daughters who are looking at suspicious books while he is distracted by advertisements.[49] As will be demonstrated in chapter 4, this scene illustrates a particular fear that is common in the discourse of challengers wherein they are afraid that other parents are not "living up to their jobs" by setting proper boundaries for their children. The image described above situates this fear within a long tradition of discourse about reading practices.

Critical Distance and Common Sense

Another concept of primary importance to understanding reading practices in the modern era is the idea of *critical distance* to a text, which is linked to the modern idea that humans are capable of rational thought and are able to apply their own ideas to a particular text. That is, they have "the capacity for resistance and disbelief" and do not simply accept whatever is written in the text.[50] This is a conceptualization of readers that defines many interpretive communities throughout the West today and it is an interpretive strategy that many librarians, administrators, and other staff of public libraries and schools share. When students are required to read a particular book in school, one surmises that the staff members who assigned it believe that the students employ both the interpretive strategies to understand the text and also maintain a critical distance from the text. In public libraries and schools, librarians and other staff members often hold parents responsible for ensuring that their children are reading materials at the appropriate level. That is, that the children are sufficiently mature to have critical distance from and maintain a rational relationship to text in the book.

In the late 18th and early 19th centuries, a particular conception of the idea of "rational thought" took hold in the United States in which rational thought is limited to "commonsense" ideas. Although it does not necessarily have resonance for many modern Americans, it is this philosophical framework that informs the discourse of challengers in this study as it helps to explain some of the intensity of challengers' actions and their position regarding the targeted books. Their discourse concerning interpretive strategies of text is grounded in a particular understanding of how one views text, wherein "rational thought" is coupled with a view of "common sense" that elevates a monosemic rather than a polysemic interpretation of text. As noted above, the fourfold sense of scripture shifted during the Reformation and interpretation became a matter of direct experience. In his monograph examining the American commonsense tradition and its major advocates including John Witherspoon and William James, Scott Philip Segrest notes that the tradition reigned in American philosophy until the post–Civil War era.[51] The American idea of common sense, which is based in a Scottish philosophical tradition, is an attitude

> grounded in experience in the sense of staying in touch with the world . . . and it is grounded by experience, in that it is the fruit of innumerable encounters with the world's basic features and innumerable judgments both of fact and logic. The common sense attitude, once highly developed, enables the clarifi-

cation, collection, and synthesis of common sense truths into a body of knowledge accessible to a broader community.[52]

Although Scottish Common Sense philosophy never became very popular on the European continent, it exerted a strong influence over the American imagination. Common sense permeates many founding documents of the United States. As Segrest persuasively argues, when the founding fathers wrote that "we hold these truths to be self-evident," they were referring to a self-evident truth that is grounded in the Scottish Common Sense tradition wherein truths must be experienced.[53]

In his monograph on the philosophical foundations and development of theology in the United States, Mark Noll argues that Common Sense philosophy provided a necessary epistemological framework for the Revolution era.[54] Previous eras including the Reformation, Puritanism of the 17th century, and the First Great Awakening of the 18th century "stressed human disability as much as human capability, noetic deficiency as much as epistemic capacity, and historical realism as much as social optimism."[55] Common Sense, on the other hand, emphasizes the self-sufficiency of individuals and their ability to observe and understand the world around them. Noll's work traces the spread of Common Sense philosophy from Scotland through the work of Scottish immigrants including John Witherspoon to institutions of higher learning in the United States, especially the College of New Jersey (later Princeton University). Of particular importance for these philosophers was an epistemology based on scientific rationality. This orientation toward the scientific, especially in the realm of the interpretation of texts, is explained in more detail by George Marsden in his writings on fundamentalism and evangelicalism in the United States.[56] According to Marsden, rational ideas based in a commonsense understanding of the world are of great importance in fundamentalist and evangelical culture. This is particularly prevalent in the idea of scientific Christianity wherein the Bible is seen as a book of scientific facts that can be understood by any reader and simply need to be rationally classified. A commonsense orientation toward reading the Bible means that

> mystical, metaphorical and symbolic perceptions of reality have largely disappeared. Instead most Americans share what sociologist Michael Cavanaugh designates an "empiricist folk epistemology." Things are thought best described exactly the way they appear, accurately with no hidden meanings.[57]

That is, when one reads the Bible—and possibly other texts—the meaning of the text is plain. In marked contrast to the fourfold sense of the scripture from the Middle Ages described above, polysemy is impossible. One example of this reading practice can be found in so-called Young Earth Creationists who do not allow for any allegorical interpretation of the Genesis 1 creation story. For them, a day *means* a 24-hour period. This viewpoint is clearly demonstrated on the website for the Young Earth Creationist group Answers in Genesis (answersingenesis.org), which states that "the Bible clearly teaches that God created in six literal, 24-hour days a few thousand years ago."

This foundation in Common Sense philosophy means that the idea of critical distance has a slightly different implication in this context. It does not necessarily refer to the idea that a *rational* interpretation of text is based in a given individual but that the *text itself* is only open to a particular interpretation—one that is self-evident to any rational reader. This study demonstrates that, for many challengers, the idea of reading a text with critical distance as an interpretive strategy is suffused with the concept of reading with common sense. The concept of reading with common sense is exceedingly important for understanding the discourse of censorship and the literalism with which challengers approach texts. Challengers often state that anyone who reads a particular text can see why they are requesting that it be removed or relocated. The problems with a particular text are self-evident and a rational person need only read it to understand this. For them, polysemy is impossible and there is only one probable interpretation for a given text. However, the manner in which this interpretation will have an effect on the reader may vary wildly depending on the mental abilities of the individual. For challengers, *it is the effects of this commonsense reading that take precedence.* Rational people (usually defined by challengers as adults) have the capacity and skill to maintain critical distance from the effects of commonsense reading while other members of society—especially children—are unable to maintain this distance. This is particularly clear when challengers discuss how the imagination operates, another idea that can be understood through past practices.

UNDISCIPLINED IMAGINATION AND MIMESIS

In his chapter on texts and images in the Renaissance, Peter Stallybrass observes that illustrations in scripture were crucial to interpreting the text. He focuses on the story of Genesis 2–3 where Adam and Eve are expelled from the garden and notes that images of the text portray them as naked while that text states that they were clothed. However, for Stallybrass, "the visual images have effectively rewritten the biblical text. These visual exegeses are more fascinating and important precisely because they produce meanings for which there is no textual support."[58] The connection between text and image is of primary importance to challengers. However, as many of the books that are the targets of challengers do not contain illustration, challengers are more often concerned with mental images that are conjured by the text on the page. That is, challengers conceptualize imagining as a mimetic experience where, through reading a text, the reader experiences the actions in the text. Since reading conjures images in one's mind, reading about a particular event is akin to living through it.

Cathy Davidson, in her monograph on the increase in novel reading in antebellum United States, describes the phenomenon as "undisciplined imagination" wherein the reader is unable to maintain distance between the events in a text and his or her own response. Davidson links fear of the undisciplined imagination to the influence of Common Sense philosophy described above. Teachers at the Ivy League colleges in the 18th century passed on to their students "an implicit suspicion of the undisciplined imagination, a conviction that literature must serve clear social needs, and a pervasive assumption that social need and social order were one and the same. Through these students—many of whom served as ministers—these ideas were readily disseminated throughout the populace."[59] This suspicion of the imagination continues to inform the discourse of challengers. They fear, as the critics in the time period that Davidson studies, that there is no space between the events in the text and the reader's response to the text. She writes that "the very act of reading fiction asserted the primacy of the reader and the legitimacy of that reader's perceptions and responses."[60] Like the critics in the 18th and 19th centuries, challengers are concerned with the effect of reading objectionable material on the maintenance of social order.

To summarize, in the modern era an orientation toward written texts developed wherein the reader maintained a critical distance toward texts. In the United States, this idea of critical distance is linked to the concept of common sense. Some people—such as in historical examples of women in the 18th and 19th centuries or children and youth in our time—are believed to be constitutionally unable to maintain critical distance toward a text. That is, the text will affect them adversely. Although challengers may disagree, it is important to note that reading practices and interpretive strategies are never isolated from one another and it is possible to read some texts with critical distance and other texts using more modular interpretive strategies. In some respects, the arguments of challengers harken back to some of the responses of the Reformation when leaders wanted their followers to read scripture on their own but were also frightened of what the consequences of this practice might be. These concepts of commonsense interpretive strategies and fear of the undisciplined imagination are an important aspect of the worldview of challengers and are key to understanding the knowledge side of the censorship equation.

WORLDVIEWS AND CHALLENGES

The metatheory of social construction, Bourdieu's theory of practice, and the historical practices of reading detailed above provide a framework for understanding the worldviews of challengers as revealed through their discourse. As noted in the introductory chapter, worldviews provide both a lens for understanding everyday life and a road map for action. Challengers' arguments and justifications for requesting the relocation, restriction, and removal of books in public institutions provide insight into their worldviews especially with regard to the state of society, the role of public school libraries in local communities, and the power of reading. Although there are other theoretical frameworks, such as childhood development and studies in children's literature, that can be employed to understand the actions of challengers, it is my contention that these frameworks do not fully explain the targeting of books in public institutions in an age of ubiquitous access to books.[61] These actions can only be understood through an analysis that explores the link between symbolic power and written knowledge. In fact, as will be demonstrated in the analysis chapters, child development and education discourse operate as what Bourdieu terms structuring structure for challengers. That is, these are the discourses on which they draw to justify their targeting of particular books. Although the cases in this study focus on literature for children, similar arguments to those found in the following analysis were made when libraries refused to buy *Fifty Shades of Grey*, an erotic book intended for adults. In keeping with their professional ethics, information professionals should always be wary when individuals argue that certain materials should be removed from the public sphere, especially when such requests are made on behalf of people who have little political agency of their own.[62]

The following chapters of the book offer an analysis of challengers' discourse using the theoretical frameworks above. Throughout these chapters the words of the challengers are shown in block quotations. Analyzed quotations are followed by a parenthetical citation indicating the quotation's source, the location of the challenge case, and date. Hearings include the gender and number of the speaker. Documents include document type and date. These quotations are exemplars of particular themes and one quotation might be used to illuminate several different concepts throughout the chapters. Except when interviewees specifically stated that I did not need to maintain confidentiality in their informed consent forms, great care is taken not to give any identifying information other than gender in the analysis. Gender is included solely for clarity and concision. All quotations are from transcripts produced by me and any errors are my own.

NOTES

1. Nelson Phillips and Cynthia Hardy, *Discourse Analysis: Investigating Processes of Social Construction* (Thousand Oaks, CA: Sage, 2002), 3.

2. Phillips and Hardy, *Discourse Analysis*, 12.

3. Peter L. Berger and Thomas Luckmann, *The Social Construction of Reality* (New York: Anchor, 1966).

4. Berger and Luckmann, *Social Construction of Reality*, 22.

5. Alfred Schutz and Thomas Luckmann, *The Structures of the Life-World* (Evanston, IL: Northwestern University Press, 1973).

6. It is called a theory of *practice* because it is midway between structuralism and subjectivism and focuses on how individuals conduct themselves within both institutional and personal constraints. In other words, the theory focuses on the practices of individuals who themselves operate in dialectical relationship between the objective and the subjective. It endeavors to explain why and how people act as if social classes actually exist even though they do not. For Bourdieu, people are neither wholly controlled by the structures of the social world nor are they only subject to their inner lives.

7. Karl Maton, "Habitus," in *Pierre Bourdieu: Key Concepts*, ed. Michael Grenfell (Durham, UK: Acumen, 2008), The concept of habitus is similar to the idea of worldview. As noted previously, a worldview is a road map for action and is the preferred term in this study. One's habitus operates in a similar fashion to a worldview as it is the embodiment of the structures that one uses for cognition and meaning in practice.

8. Pierre Bourdieu, *Outline of a Theory of Practice* (New York: Cambridge University Press, 1987).

9. Pierre Bourdieu, "The Forms of Capital," in *Handbook of Theory and Research for the Sociology of Education*, ed. John G. Richardson (Westport, CT: Greenwood, 1986), 241.

10. Bourdieu, *Outline of a Theory of Practice*, 183.

11. Pierre Bourdieu, *Language and Symbolic Power* (Cambridge, MA: Harvard University Press, 1991).

12. Pierre Bourdieu, "The Social Space and the Genesis of Groups," *Theory and Society* 14, no. 6 (1985): 734. The term "violence" refers to the domination of one social group with greater symbolic capital and power over another group that has less symbolic capital and power. Although this violence takes place in the realm of the symbolic, it is still a real form of suffering, as it affects how a particular group is able to live out their lives.

13. James LaRue, *The New Inquisition: Understanding and Managing Intellectual Freedom Challenges* (Westport, CT: Libraries Unlimited, 2007), 51. This is an important point. Although the majority of the challengers in this study are from the right, there are also left-wing challenges of books. Many of these focus on the effects of stereotyping on readers.

14. Martyn Lyons, *A History of Reading and Writing in the Western World* (New York: Palgrave Macmillan, 2010).

15. David Finkelstein and Alistair McCleery, *An Introduction to Book History* (New York: Routledge, 2005), 40.

16. For more on Peirce's theory of signs see Albert Atkin, "Peirce's Theory of Signs," in *The Stanford Encyclopedia of Philosophy*, ed. Edward N. Zalta, Summer 2013 ed., http://plato.stanford.edu/archives/sum2013/entries/peirce-semiotics/.

17. Ellen Seiter, "Semiotics, Structuralism, and Television," in *Channels of Discourse, Reassembled: Television and Contemporary Criticism*, ed. Robert C. Allen, 2nd ed. (Chapel Hill: University of North Carolina Press, 1992), 36.

18. Lisa Jardine, "The Triumph of the Book," in *Worldly Goods* (New York: Norton, 1998), 177.

19. Robert Darnton, *The Business of Enlightenment: A Publishing History of the 'Encyclopédie,' 1775–1800* (Cambridge, MA: Belknap, 1979).

20. William J. Gilmore, *Reading Becomes a Necessity of Life: Material and Cultural Life in Rural New England, 1780–1835* (Knoxville: University of Tennessee Press, 1989).

21. Louise S. Robbins, *The Dismissal of Miss Ruth Brown: Civil Rights, Censorship, and the American Library* (Norman: University of Oklahoma Press, 2001), 160.

22. Elizabeth L. Eisenstein, *The Printing Revolution in Early Modern Europe*, 2nd ed. (Cambridge, UK: Cambridge University Press, 2005).

23. Adrian Johns, *The Nature of the Book: Print and Knowledge in the Making*, 1st ed. (Chicago: University of Chicago Press, 2000).

24. Daniel Selcer, *Philosophy and the Book: Early Modern Figures of Material Inscription* (New York: Continuum, 2010), 188.

25. Selcer, *Philosophy and the Book*, 192.

26. Elizabeth Long, "Textual Interpretation as Collective Action," in *The Ethnography of Reading*, ed. J. Boyarin (Berkeley: University of California Press, 1992), 180–211.

27. It must be noted that this overview has a distinctly Christian and Western bent. However, as the majority religion in the West during the time periods described, these are the practices most studied by researchers. For a description of Jewish reading practices during the Middle Ages, see Robert Bonfil, "Reading in the Jewish Communities of Western Europe in the Middle Ages," in *A History of Reading in the West*, ed. Guglielmo Cavallo and Roger Chartier (Amherst: University of Massachusetts Press, 2003), 149–78. For more on the history of the book and reading in the East, see individual national histories in *The Book: A Global History*, edited by Michael F. Suarez, S.J., and J. R. Woudhuysen. New York, NY: Oxford, 2013.

28. Stanley Eugene Fish, *Is There a Text in This Class?* (Cambridge, MA: Harvard University Press, 1982), 168.

29. Roger Chartier, "The Practical Impact of Writing," in *The Book History Reader*, ed. David Finkelstein and Alistair McCleery (New York: Routledge, 2002), 157–81.

30. Lyons, *History of Reading and Writing*, 13.

31. M. B. Parkes, "Reading, Copying and Interpreting a Text in the Early Middle Ages," in *A History of Reading in the West*, ed. Guglielmo Cavallo and Roger Chartier (Amherst: University of Massachusetts Press, 2003), 90–102.

32. Jacqueline Hamesse, "The Scholastic Model of Reading," in *A History of Reading in the West*, ed. Guglielmo Cavallo and Roger Chartier (Amherst: University of Massachusetts Press, 2003), 108.

33. Hamesse, "Scholastic Model of Reading," 104.

34. Paul Saenger, "Reading in the Later Middle Ages," in *A History of Reading in the West*, ed. Guglielmo Cavallo and Roger Chartier (Amherst: University of Massachusetts Press, 2003), 137.

35. Brian Stock, *Listening for the Text* (Baltimore: Johns Hopkins University Press, 1996), 23.

36. Anthony Grafton, "The Humanist as Reader," in *A History of Reading in the West*, ed. Guglielmo Cavallo and Roger Chartier (Amherst: University of Massachusetts Press, 2003), 179–212.

37. Grafton, "Humanist as Reader," 204.

38. Robert Mullin, *A Short World History of Christianity* (Louisville, KY: Westminster John Knox Press, 2008).

39. Jean-François Gilmont, "Protestant Reformations and Reading," in *A History of Reading in the West*, ed. Guglielmo Cavallo and Roger Chartier (Amherst: University of Massachusetts Press, 2003), 213–37.

40. Gilmont, "Protestant Reformations and Reading," 226.

41. Lyons, *History of Reading and Writing*, 55.

42. Jardine, "Triumph of the Book."

43. Finkelstein and McCleery, *Introduction to Book History*; Lyons, *History of Reading and Writing*.

44. Lyons, *History of Reading and Writing*.

45. Gilmore, *Reading Becomes a Necessity of Life*.

46. Cathy Davidson, *Revolution and the Word: The Rise of the Novel in America*, expanded ed. (New York: Oxford University Press, 2004), 54.

47. Gilmore, *Reading Becomes a Necessity of Life*.

48. Leah Price, "Reading: The State of the Discipline," *Book History* 7 (2004): 318.

49. Stephen Colclough, *Consuming Texts: Readers and Reading Communities, 1695–1870* (New York: Palgrave Macmillan, 2007).

50. Lyons, *History of Reading and Writing*, 117.

51. Scott Philip Segrest, *America and the Political Philosophy of Common Sense* (Columbia: University of Missouri Press, 2010).

52. Segrest, *America and the Political Philosophy*, 23.

53. Segrest, *America and the Political Philosophy*, 6.

54. Mark Noll, *America's God: From Jonathan Edwards to Abraham Lincoln* (New York: Oxford University Press, 2002).

55. Noll, *America's God*, 95.

56. George Marsden, *Understanding Fundamentalism and Evangelicalism* (Grand Rapids, MI: Eerdmans, 1991).

57. Marsden, *Understanding Fundamentalism*, 157.

58. Peter Stallybrass, "Visible and Invisible Letters: Text versus Image in Renaissance England and Europe," in *Visible Writings: Cultures, Forms, Readings*, ed. Marija Dalbello and Mary Lewis Shaw (New Brunswick, NJ: Rutgers University Press, 2011), 87.

59. Davidson, *Revolution and the Word*, 114.

60. Davidson, *Revolution and the Word*, 118.

61. For examples of works in these fields that address some of the issues raised in the study, see Kerry H. Robinson, *Innocence, Knowledge, and the Construction of Childhood: The Contradictory Nature of Sexuality and Censorship in Children's Contemporary Lives* (London: Routledge, 2013); Alyson Miller, "Unsuited for Age Group: The Scandals of Children's Literature," *College Literature: A Journal of Critical Literary Studies* 41, no. 2 (April 1, 2014): 120–40; and Herbert R. Kohl, *Should We Burn Babar? Essays on Children's Literature and the Power of Stories* (New York: New Press, 1995).

62. Bill Thompson, "County Library Shuns '50 Shades of Grey,'" *Ocala (FL) Star-Banner*, May 15, 2012, http://docs.newsbank.com.proxy2.library.illinois.edu/s/InfoWeb/aggdocs/AWNB/13ED04E00DD58100/0D0CB57DF8A1C275?s_lang.

Chapter Three

Perfect Timing

The e-mails, tweets, and posts came in all week: "Did you hear about this?" "*Invisible Man* was banned in North Carolina!?" "Did you see what happened in North Carolina?" Since I have a Google Alert for banned books (among other intellectual freedom topics) sent to my e-mail every day, I had heard about this particular incident prior to my friends and family contacting me. However, the banning caught my attention due to a trend that I had noticed recently. Since the early 2010s with the implementation of the federally led and state-implemented Common Core standards in public schools across the country, more and more books by people of color have been challenged in public schools. The Common Core is an attempt to normalize curricula and outcomes across the country and includes both English Language Arts and Mathematics standards, and its implementation has been controversial on both the political right and left. As part of the Language Arts standards, the Common Core includes several lists of recommended books for students.[1] When one reads through the lists, it is clear that the developers of the standards attempted to diversify their recommendations and included many books by people of color including *Dragonwings* by Laurence Yep and *The Bluest Eye* by Toni Morrison. Although books by people of color have slowly been included in the canon, the lists included works that were not previously part of elementary and secondary school curricula in the United States. This inclusion seems to correlate with a notable increase in the number of books by people of color being challenged in public schools. The list of "Most Frequently Challenged Authors of the 21st Century" from the ALA includes more authors of color after 2010 when the Common Core was first implemented.[2] Although *Invisible Man*, Ralph Ellison's novel on the African American experience first published in 1947, is not on the federal Common

Core text exemplars list, the circumstances of the challenge were similar to those I had noticed over the prior year or so.

Invisible Man, along with two other books about race in America—*Black Like Me* by John Howard Griffin and *Passing* by Nella Larsen—was included as a recommended book on the 2013 summer reading list for juniors at Randleman High School in Randleman, North Carolina. After her child brought the book home, a parent took exception to its inclusion, calling the book "not so innocent" and formally requested that the book be removed from the school's library.[3] Although, as will be demonstrated in this chapter, the challenger's arguments against the book's inclusion were similar to others found in challenge cases, one unusual aspect of this case was the timing. The Randolph County School Board voted for the ban on September 16, one week before the 2013 celebration of Banned Books Week was scheduled to begin.

THEY BANNED *INVISIBLE MAN*?

Every year during the last full week of September, the American Library Association's Office for Intellectual Freedom sponsors Banned Books Week. The celebration is intended to highlight books that are challenged in the United States and celebrate the freedom to read. The coincidence of timing (Banned Books Week would begin on September 22) along with the reputation of *Invisible Man* as a classic work of American literature proved irresistible to the press. The local paper for Randleman out of Asheboro, North Carolina, reported that a Google search revealed "pages and pages" of stories on the case and that a news story had appeared on Russian television.[4] The general tone of most of the articles, blog posts, and so forth, was one of disbelief—how could a school board ban a definitive work on racial injustice like *Invisible Man*?

This chapter attempts to answer that question by tracing the timeline of the North Carolina *Invisible Man* case and exploring the arguments used to justify the book's banning. It begins with an overview of the social and political climate in North Carolina at the time, including the rise of conservatism and the implementation of the Common Core in the state's public schools. The second half of the chapter is a timeline of the *Invisible Man* case. Interspersed throughout these overviews are the arguments that the challenger and board members employed to justify the removal of the book from public school libraries. These arguments come from two sources: an interview with one of the board members and documents related to the case from the school board. Using the method of analysis described in the Methodological Note (appendix A) these arguments were analyzed for common themes that are found in many contemporary challenge cases around the

United States. More specifically, the arguments centered on the role of public institutions in the community in providing reading material and the effect of commonsense interpretive strategies on youth's moral development. The chapter also includes quotations of an interview with the president of the local NAACP. These provide more context for the political situation in the area and the events of the case.

As part of my research I try to attend challenge hearings whenever it is feasible. Often this is quite difficult as they are usually announced the day before they are held. For the *Invisible Man* case, my teaching schedule allowed me to travel from Illinois to North Carolina on September 25, the day that the board reconsidered its vote to ban the book. While at the board meeting, I took fieldnotes (see appendix A) and recorded the session. The meeting was very short (around 45 minutes) and after the final vote some members of the board lingered a bit in the meeting room. I then approached several of the board members and asked if they were interested in giving me an interview on the challenge case. One school board member, Tracy Boyles, responded positively to my invitation for an interview. After getting Mr. Boyles's information, I went outside and noticed that there were several reporters talking to a group of people on the sidewalk. The primary respondent to the press was Donald Matthews, the president of the Randolph County NAACP. After he spoke to reporters, I approached him and asked if

Figure 3.1.   Randolph County (NC) Board of Education Meeting, September 25, 2013. *James P. Capers*

he would be interested in an interview and he agreed. Quotations from both interviews are included throughout the rest of the chapter.

More broadly, this chapter is intended to provide some background for understanding how book challenges arise in early 21st-century America by discussing the particular social and political context for one challenge case. Such detailed context is not included in the following chapters, which focus more on the common themes found in the discourse of challengers rather than the background of individual challenge cases. It is hoped that by providing an overview of the context for one case, the themes in the following chapters will be situated more fully within the social and political frameworks of the United States in the early 21st century. The case in North Carolina, in some respects, presents a microcosm of the societal conflicts of contemporary America as they play out in a small community that is undergoing significant changes.

BACKLASH IN NORTH CAROLINA

Barack Obama, a black Democrat, won the presidential electoral vote in North Carolina in 2008. Prior to his win, no Democrat had won North Carolina's electoral votes since 1976 when a Southern white evangelical Christian, Jimmy Carter, was on the ballot. In spite of this long history of voting Republican in federal elections, North Carolina has long been considered a bit of an anomaly in the South. For example, even though the state's most famous politician was the long-serving right-wing U.S. senator Jesse Helms, moderate Democrats had dominated North Carolina since Reconstruction. This began to change in the later part of the first decade of the 2000s and then reached a tipping point in 2010. This transformation is, of course, the result of many different factors; however, two primary ones center on the efforts of one man, Art Pope, and the infusion of so-called dark money into state politics. As reported in the *American Prospect*, prior to 2008 North Carolina saw a marked shift in its demographic makeup starting in the 1960s. An influx of people of color, particularly African Americans migrating back to the South and Latino/as moving to the area, led to gains in the overall number of people in the state who usually voted Democratic. The Research Triangle, situated in an area that includes the cities of Raleigh, Durham, and Chapel Hill and the three institutions of higher education, also drew workers who tended to be more politically liberal to the state.[5] These two populations increased the number of liberal and moderate voters in the state since nonnative whites and people of color tended to vote Democratic in local and federal elections. However, in spite of these demographic changes, North Carolina politics shifted hard to the right following the election of Barack Obama in 2008. An article in the *New Yorker* that focuses on Art Pope, a wealthy political donor, and the influence on the state's politics gives some idea as to how this shift occurred.[6] Starting with the midterm elections in 2010, Ed Gillespie, a Republican operative, attempted to implement his Redistricting Majority Project (REDMAP) across the United States by staging a Republican takeover of state legislatures across the country. In North Carolina, Art Pope helped Gillespie's campaign by providing the initial financing for two political groups, Real Jobs North Carolina and Civitas Action. According to the *American Prospect*, Pope's agenda was well known in North Carolina: "scale back taxes, take away the social safety net, and reverse focus on public schools."[7] The two Pope groups financed attack ads against vulnerable Democrats in the state legislature. With the financial backing from Pope's organizations, Republicans won 18 of the 22 targeted seats.

Now that the state legislature and governorship was controlled by the Republican Party, the policy trajectory of North Carolina turned hard to the right. After years of moderate and progressive policy implementation, including support for financing clean elections and long early voting times, the new legislature passed bills that overturned clean elections and implemented onerous voting identification laws. Following the completion of the 2010 census, the legislature also oversaw a redistricting process that placed all Democrats in the state into three (out of a total 13) congressional districts. In the midst of all these policy changes, Art Pope became cocounsel to the state legislature. Unfortunately, his official position in state politics has made it difficult to investigate his involvement in the changes, as all of his work is subject to attorney-client privilege. The Republican-led legislature also began to take over local municipalities by passing bills that would keep Democratic-led cities from leading themselves. Even though these changes were sweeping, the left attempted to respond even though they no longer held political power in the legislature. One well-known response is the demonstrations, known as Moral Mondays, that began in April of 2013 and take place outside the state legislature every Monday.

Although the events described above present a high-level view of the political changes in North Carolina, they provide some context for both the challenge case in Randolph County and the cases discussed in the following chapters. The reactionary policy changes in response to shifts in the population in North Carolina can be found throughout states and communities in the United States. There seems to be a correlation between the so-called browning of America and the election of an African American to the highest office of the land, with a sense of unease throughout some segments of society.[8] The country is becoming something different than what it was before, and some are unsure how to react to these changes. Even though the reaction to the demographic changes in North Carolina have occurred somewhat later than in other areas of the country, the so-called culture wars have been a part of America's political and social landscape since the 1980s. As described by

James Davison Hunter, the culture wars are a struggle to define America through a conflict that is marked by a polarization of ideologies.[9] It is important to note that U.S. society has changed in immeasurable ways since the 1960s and, in some respects, the legislative reaction in North Carolina is a direct outcome of these changes; and, as will be demonstrated in this chapter and those that follow, challenge cases are another outcome. Book challenge cases, similar to other events of local politics, are the embodiment of community control over public institutions. In Randolph County, which incorporates the town of Randleman and is the site of the *Invisible Man* challenge, there is strong evidence of the reactionary politics that can be found throughout North Carolina and other parts of the country.

RANDOLPH COUNTY, NORTH CAROLINA, AND THE COMMON CORE

Randolph County is in the Piedmont area in the center of North Carolina. Its county seat and largest town, Asheboro, is about 30 miles to the south of Greensboro and about 70 miles northwest of Charlotte. According to the U.S. Census, in 2010 it had a total population of 141,752 and was 5.8 percent black and 10.4 percent Hispanic or Latino. By contrast, in 2000, the total population was 130,454 and was 5.6 percent black and 6.6 percent Hispanic or Latino. All the local officials in the county are Republicans and, according to Donald Matthews, the president of the Randolph County NAACP, all are white. Both the state representatives and state senator for the area ran unopposed in 2010. The county commissioner faced a write-in challenge but won handily. Three school board seats were also elected in 2010 in a nonpartisan election. In the interview, Donald Matthews stated that

> Randolph Country is probably one of the most racist counties that I've ever lived in. I'm the product of a military father and I'm in the military myself so I've lived in quite a few places but no place like this. This is a very strange place. There are no elected public officials of color here. In Randolph County period and there are probably 10 or 12 municipalities. Their . . . even in their hiring process in the hospital or community college—two of the biggest employers—there're no people of color in administration. Teachers dotted here and there . . . couple of nurses here and there. People in housekeeping. But people that actually make policy . . . you don't have that in this county. (Interview with D. Matthews, October 9, 2013)

Although this is the opinion of one person, it is clear that there is systemic underrepresentation of people of color in Randolph County. This assertion is corroborated when one examines the pictures of commissioners and board members on the local government website. For example, the school board is made up of six men and one woman, all of whom are white.

The state of North Carolina adopted the Common Core as part of its Standard Course of Study in 2012. *Invisible Man* is listed as a suggested book for English III and IV. The Guidelines for Teachers state that *Invisible Man* should be used to "understand how American culture has sought to balance individual rights with the common good," an "Essential Standard" for the culture unit. *Invisible Man* is used to explain how "literature, philosophy, and the arts can provide varying perspectives on freedom, justice and equality" by showing that these ideas are not universal. Suggestions for other books for the standard include Hector St. John de Crevecoeur's *Letters from an American Farmer* and information on the women's, Chicago, American Indian, and civil rights movements.[10] As noted above, *Invisible Man* was added to the Randleman High School summer reading list in 2013 for juniors. Randleman High School, which is located in the north of the county, is a small school of around 900 students. The school's population is 73 percent white, 19 percent Hispanic, and 5 percent black, and in the 2012–2013 school year 39.3 percent of the white students, 37.8 percent of the black, and 27.1 percent of the Hispanic students passed their end-of-course exams.[11] One would guess that the summer reading list went out to parents and students sometime in June of 2013. On July 10, the superintendent of schools, Dr. Stephen Gainey, received a call from a concerned parent of a Randleman High School student.

BANNING *INVISIBLE MAN*

Although most of the world first heard about the banning of *Invisible Man* in September of 2013, the case actually started that summer. According to Randolph County Board of Education documents, although the parent contacted Superintendent Gainey on July 10, he was not informed of the parent's challenge until he talked to her on July 18. A memo from the assistant superintendent, Catherine Berry, notes that Dr. Gainey called the parent and left messages several times between her initial call on July 10 and when he was able to speak with her on the 18th. The memo also states that the principal of Randleman High left six messages for the parent between July 18 and July 25 both to discuss the parent's concern regarding the book and inform her of the formal process for challenging curriculum materials. At the end of July, the parent sent her completed request for reconsideration form and supplemental material to the principal. Donald Matthews provides a bit more information about the challenger:

> The young lady who asked the book to be banned was an African American female. And she wanted it banned because she didn't think it was suitable for her child to read. And they had three other choices and that's what the superintendent, the school principal and the teacher informed her that [if] she did not

want that book to be read by her child then there were two other choices for
her to choose from but she homed in on just that one book and proceeded to
submit the paperwork to the school board to get the book banned. (Interview
with D. Matthews, October 9, 2013)

The challenger's initial request stated that the book should be pulled from the
school library because "chapters 2, 3, 24—Speak in detail of sexual encounters, incest and etc."[12] She attached 12 pages of supplemental material with
quotations from the book to her request with commentary sprinkled throughout.

The Reconsideration Form

Randolph County uses a standard request for reconsideration form that asks
several different questions about the material that the challenger would like
to be evaluated. Like many challengers, she focuses on the idea that the book
is too advanced for the intended audience. For example, the challenger uses
an interesting turn of phrase in response to the question "What do you believe is the purpose of this material?" She writes that "the narrator writes in
the first person emphasizing his individual experience and his feelings about
the events portrayed in his life. This novel is not innocent; instead this book
is filthier [*sic*], too much for teenagers" (Request for reconsideration, Randleman, NC, July 30, 2013). The use of the term "innocent" is telling here
and seems to indicate that the author had an underhanded purpose for telling
his story. This criticism that the book is not "innocent" is also repeated in the
supplemental material. Unfortunately, the challenger does not clearly answer
the question "What do you feel might be the result of a student using this
material?" and simply replies that "this is not age appropriate reading material for the youngest of your student body," which avoids the question. The
challenger's supplementary material is also revealing when she states that the
board must take parents' role as boundary setters with regard to moral
knowledge into consideration when choosing books for the curriculum: "You
must respect all religions and point of views [*sic*] when it comes to the
parents and what they feel is age appropriate for their young children to read,
without their knowledge." Following this brief summary of her complaints
about the book, the challenger provides summaries of much of the book,
highlighting its sexually graphic passages.

This tactic of highlighting problematic passages is common to many challengers and speaks to their understanding of the power of reading. The *Invisible Man* challenger states that "in this book, this man doesn't just mention,
he actually goes into great detail about sexual encounters" (Request for reconsideration, Randleman, NC, July 30, 2013). As will be discussed in the
following chapters, challengers often discuss reading as a mimetic and embodied practice. That is, when people read a text, they actually experience

events along with the narrator. As the challenger in the North Carolina case states after describing a rape scene in the book, "And this is just one of two times so far, that this writer goes into too much information about him and rape." It is clear that, for this challenger, this assessment of the text is true at face value—the words "mean what they say and say what they mean." Like many challengers, she does not allow for any other interpretations of the text other than her own commonsense strategy. The pages of quotations are presented without commentary as it is assumed that the reader will simply agree with the challenger's analysis of the text. Using a commonsense interpretive strategy, the challenger indicates that words on the page speak for themselves.

The challenger ends her initial request by restating her original complaint and requests that the book be removed from the summer reading list and library shelves:

> This book should not be on the summer reading list, especially when [you] know that most parents would not review this book first, before handing it over to their 15–16 year old child. . . . This book is freely in your library for them to read. And clearly, no one truly read through this book before they allowed it to be [placed] where young teenagers could freely check it out of your library. (Request for reconsideration, Randleman, NC, July 30, 2013)

For her, the problems with the book are self-evident and the remedy—to remove the book—is clear. She goes on to state that if the book was reviewed then the problem resides with the reviewers. If there is "appropriate staff of people" the books will be "more age appropriate" and "this new staff/group will not choose such vile books for a young child to read without their parent's knowledge." One might say that the challenger is arguing that those who chose to include the book cannot "read." This accusation is indicative to monosemic interpretive strategies—for the challenger, there are no alternative ways to understand the meaning of the text.

Committee Meetings

In keeping with board policy, the school's media specialist assembled an ad hoc School Media Advisory Committee to review the book. The committee consisted of the school's assistant principal, a lead teacher, an Exceptional Children teacher, an English teacher, the English Department chair, and the school media specialist. The committee's report, dated August 6, reiterates *Invisible Man*'s status as a literary classic and that it should not be pulled from the library. The committee writes that the book "has appeared more than any other novel as a free response option for the AP Literature and Composition Examination between 1971 and 2013; most recently it has been a choice the last six years in a row."[13] The committee states that the book was cited on the North Carolina Department of Public Instruction Instructional Support Tools discussed above and also was part of the North Carolina Standard Course of Study. It also notes that the book was a winner of the 1953 National Book Award and is listed by the Library of Congress as one of the "Books That Shaped America."

The committee report also includes recommendations for improving procedures for summer reading lists. First, synopses of all the books will be provided along with disclaimers regarding possibly objectionable subject matter. The books should also be listed in order of difficulty. Second, all the selections will be reviewed by two non-English teachers. The review committee will then discuss the book and write a synopsis and disclaimer. The parent received notice of the committee's decision on August 6 and called the superintendent the same day.

According to the memo from the assistant superintendent, the parent notified Dr. Gainey of her intention to appeal the decision of the school-based committee. This escalated the case to district level and the superintendent appointed a Central Services Committee to review the book. Although this initial appeal was made verbally, the parent sent a written request that was received by the district on August 13. This request, similar to the first one, notes that she is particularly concerned that parents will not be aware of the explicitness of the book:

> The book is still inside the school library and it's available for other children to continue reading, along with them speaking on explicit subject matters in class, that their parents are not aware of once school begins this school year, 2013–2014. The students still have to write a journal on this book, then write a report after school begins, and the topics will be discussed in class. . . . This is disappointing. They have waited so long anyway, that the children have now read, or came across this book for the summer to read, and the parents are still unaware of the explicit content and language within the text—the brothels, the detailed incest, the rapes. Not even an automated phone call to the parent's homes, warning the parents this summer has been done. (Reconsideration appeal, Randleman, NC, received August 13, 2013)

Like other challengers, she states that books like *Invisible Man* should not be discussed in school and is concerned that teachers have some sort of prurient interest in the book if they are willing to discuss such topics out loud with their students. The challenger is also concerned that the decision to retain the book was made by a "few staff members" and that a "simple five-man vote amongst school officials/teachers should not have books like this allowed, slipped into our school libraries for our children [to] freely read, and then the topic of brothels, detailed incest, and wanted rapes are then discussed in classrooms" (reconsideration appeal, Randleman, NC, received August 13, 2013).This touches on another common theme throughout challengers' discourse: that the process for evaluating books is opaque and that sometimes the decision is based on the opinions of very few people.

As noted above, in response to the challenger's appeal, the superintendent convened an ad hoc District Media Advisory Committee, which consisted of ten district employees including the director of media and technology and the director of middle school instruction. As with the school-based committee, the Central Services Committee recommended keeping the book in the library. The Media Advisory Committee was tasked with answering the question "Did the book have curricular value?" (reconsideration appeal, Randleman, NC, received August 13, 2013). The memo from the committee noted that "parts of the book were not pleasant" but these were not predominant throughout the text. The committee also discussed the idea that "'life' is not always pleasant" and that the book is an accurate portrayal of the pre–civil rights era in the United States.[14] The official memo with the decision to keep the book in the library was sent to the challenger on August 15. This decision was then presented to the school board.

The Board Meeting and Response

As noted above, the Randolph County School Board is made up of six men and one woman who all serve for four-year terms. Like many school boards across the country, the board consists of prominent members of the community at large, including a retired police chief and the current fire chief. Also similar to other school boards, no educators serve on the board. The school board met on August 20 but, according to the agenda for the day, did not discuss the *Invisible Man* case. The case was discussed at the following meeting on September 15 as a "recommendation to address parent complaint about the book entitled *Invisible Man* by Ralph Ellison." It was at this meeting that the board banned the book on a 5–2 vote. According to news accounts in the *Asheboro (North Carolina) Courier-Tribune*, one of the board members noted that the book was "a hard read" while another stated that he "didn't find any literary value" and was "for not allowing it to be available."[15] According to Mr. Boyles, the board member whom I was able to interview, many of the members had not read the entire book before this vote.

Mr. Boyles, who had been on the school board for approximately 10 months before the challenge case, initially voted to remove the book from the school libraries. He noted that he was not familiar with the book at the beginning of the challenge and read only the first couple of chapters before the first vote. As will be discussed in the following chapters, throughout challengers' discourse there is an acute sense that ideas in books should be true and "good." In particular, he stated that he was concerned that the presence of obscene language in the book meant that such language was condoned by the school board:

> I don't like the, you know, the kids to pick up on something and they say well it's written down in a book the school system says we can read this book so it's alright for me to go to my classroom and curse and you know and stuff like that. I mean. For me, I thought it was pretty much saying so this is okay. (Interview with T. Boyles, September 27, 2013)

Here Mr. Boyles argues that because the book has bad language and has been recommended by the school system, then students will believe that cursing is acceptable behavior. By implication, all books found in the school's curriculum should contain "true" knowledge. Here it is possible to see how writing is an indexical sign as described in chapter 2. Mr. Boyles is arguing that there should be a clear connection between the text and "truth" in the real world.

The vote to remove the book from school libraries set off a media frenzy across the country and the world. Banned Books Week started the following week, and the board members received e-mails and phone calls from all over the world. Mr. Boyles stated that

> some of them were kind of vulgar. You know they called us ignorant . . . [unclear] . . . we didn't know what we was doing. And on [the] local level, talking to a few people . . . you know . . . they just thought we . . . they were real cordial. In their emails they explained to us that this is [a] great piece of literature and all. But a lot of the emails we received from out of state, they wasn't professional. They called us a bunch of backwoods hicks and stuff like that, I mean, it wasn't good. (Interview with T. Boyles, September 27, 2013)

Mr. Boyles implies that the e-mails in the latter category were not very effective in persuading him to change his mind regarding banning the book. He noted that he did not respond to any of the e-mails that he received.

After hearing about the banning, Donald Matthews and the local NAACP also responded to the ban. Mr. Matthews stated that he found out as much as he could about the challenger and worked to make sure that the organization's response was respectful of her role as a parent:

> Subsequently, the calls went out and the calls to arms came and . . . I had mixed emotions. I really wanted to make sure Number 1: that this young lady understood that I was not against her right to choose for her child. But I was against her right to choose for my child. And that's where our stance was and actually did several other interviews I wanted to make that clear to her from the very front. That we were not against her right because . . . as a matter of fact I applauded her for being involved in her school and her child's education. (Interview with D. Matthews, October 9, 2013)

The organization posted an open letter to the board from Mr. Matthews on its Facebook page, stating that it found it "very offensive that you would even consider such a move as to ban a book of this stature."[16] The letter also noted that the members of the organization were discouraged that the board members did not take the recommendations of the committees into account when they made their decision and also that there was no time for public comment at the meeting. In response to the furor, the board called a special meeting for September 25, right in the middle of Banned Books Week.

Reinstated

As noted earlier, I was able to attend the meeting on September 25. It began with the board attorney discussing the legal framework for removing the book. First, she noted that she had not realized that the September 16 discussion would result in a vote on a motion to remove the book. It was her understanding that the recommendation on the agenda was simply to schedule a hearing for the book. She also noted that school libraries operate as a "marketplace for ideas" within the school system. The assistant superintendent of curriculum and instruction discussed the review process for *Invisible Man* and then two high school teachers discussed how they employed the book in their classes. The board then offered arguments for and against keeping the book. Although the original challenger was not present, the assistant superintendent read a statement from her, which stated that "school libraries are not public libraries and shouldn't have materials that are not appropriate for students 15 years old or younger." Finally the board voted 6–1 to reinstate the book to school libraries.

Mr. Boyles discussed why he changed his vote during our interview. He is quoted at length for clarity:

> You know, I'd say on the ride home that evening, I thought to myself you know we didn't really do what we should have. We [the board] really didn't investigate this book like [we] should have. I take my blame with it. I just got to thinking . . . I've always said, you know, it's not my job as a school board member to raise people's children. It's their job to raise their children with their morals and their values in school. And I got to thinking about . . . got to talking to someone about all of the other books our libraries carry. Some of them I read when I was in school. If you really set down and look at those books and you want to think if you want to nitpick we would have to take about a third of our books out of our libraries. So I mean we got *The Scarlet Letter*, we read that in high school, [that's] adultery. So there's great works of literature out there has . . . if you base your personal opinions on it. You know you could remove them if you wanted to. And I thought, like I said at the board meeting, I thought about my son in the military. He fighting for freedom of speech and democracy and everything and I said I'm just going against what he's doing. And really after we started receiving the emails from people it

really opened your eyes and I said did I look at this book like I should have.
No I didn't. A lot of times it takes the good with the bad to really come out
with a good answer to something and sometimes you have to take a little bad
for the greater good. And you have to really overlook some things to get the
full justice of something. (Interview with T. Boyles, September 27, 2013)

Here Mr. Boyles echoes some of the common arguments that librarians
and other information professionals give to justify free access to resources in
libraries, including that it is the parents' responsibility to monitor their children's reading. He also notes that he read books about objectionable themes
but this did not necessarily change his overall moral worldview. Here we see
a shift in his assumption and use of a monosemic interpretive strategy to a
polysemic interpretive strategy—one wherein the effects of reading a particular book are unknown.[17] Mr. Boyles also stated that he read the entire book
before the second vote and that although he did not agree with the language
and obscenity, the book did have value.

AFTERMATH

The challenge case to *Invisible Man* in Randolph County was a whirlwind
and ended almost as suddenly as it began. Only one board member did not
change his vote to remove the book from public school libraries. *Invisible
Man* was reinstated to the recommended reading list and media attention
moved on. Mr. Matthews mentioned that membership in the county NAACP
increased from 50 to 115, and he called the book challenge a "shot in the
arm" to the African American community in the county. Unlike some challenges, there have not been reports in the media of lingering resentment from
community members over the reinstatement of the book. If one judges by the
letters to the editor in the *Asheboro Courier-Tribune* at the time of the challenge, very few members of the community supported the challenger in her
campaign to ban *Invisible Man*.

Like all challenge cases, the case against *Invisible Man* demonstrates the
relationship between power and knowledge. One can see how the inclusion
of a particular book as part of a national impetus to change educational
standards had an effect on a small town in North Carolina where an individual attempted to use her power over a local public institution to block access to
the knowledge contained in the book. The parent makes pointed arguments
about the "not so innocent" book, stating that it has the power to damage
young minds. She expects that these arguments will be taken at face value by
presenting the text from the novel. There is no room for other interpretations
of this text; only her commonsense one can be employed by the reader. In the
following chapters, instead of focusing on one case, the arguments employed
by challengers in several cases, many of which are similar to those found in

Chapter Four

The Moral Decline of Society, Institutions, and the Family

One of the most well-known challenge cases in the past 10 years took place in Lewiston, Maine. In 2007, a concerned grandmother checked out *It's Perfectly Normal: Changing Bodies, Growing Up, Sex, and Sexual Health*, a children's sexual education book by Robie Harris, and refused to return it. The grandmother described the book as "extremely offensive to the dignity of person hood [*sic*]" (Letter to the board, Lewiston, ME, August 11, 2007). She was presented with a civil summons and had to appear before a judge where she was informed that she was in danger of going to jail for community property theft. The grandmother pleaded guilty to the charge, but eventually the charges were dropped because the judge did not want to make her a martyr to the cause. The judge ordered her to pay a $100 fine and return the books. The case eventually petered out. Even though *It's Perfectly Normal* has long been one of the most challenged books in the country, the idea of a grandmother being arrested for stealing a sex education book was tantalizing to the media. *Jezebel*, *Boing Boing*, and other non-library-related media covered the story with relish. *Jezebel*, for example, referenced the television show *The Simpsons* and noted that they were "feeling a Nelson Muntz–style *HaHa* in [their] heads right now."[1]

Even though she became the object of ridicule in much of the media, the grandmother took her challenge very seriously. She checked out *It's Perfectly Normal* from both the Lewiston and nearby Auburn Public Libraries and did not intend to ever return them. Instead of returning the books, she sent a letter to the administrations of both libraries explaining her actions and checks for $20.95 (the cost plus tax) to purchase the book. Through the course of the challenge case, the concerned grandmother sent several letters to the administration of the local public library in Lewiston. These missives capture several of the common themes in challengers' discourse that will be discussed in this chapter, particularly her concern regarding the decline of society, the role of public institutions, the perceived lack of parental involvement in their children's lives, and the preservation of children's innocence. In the following quotation, note that the challenger uses the initialisms LPL and IPN for the Lewiston Public Library and the book in question, *It's Perfectly Normal*, respectively. SIECUS is the Sexuality Information and Education Council of the United States, an education, policy, and advocacy organization based out of New York. The idiosyncratic spacing is the challenger's own:

> A nation wars against its own people when it fails to defend the essence of masculinity and femininity. Yes it is a political maneuver for the L P L to accept and defend "I P N" to be on its shelves: L P L is guilty of a whole lot more than violating the City of Lewiston's Obscenity Codes, but in my defense of not guilty I will give some evidences that L P L conjoins with the SIECUS curricula and Planned Parenthood to destroy our great nation. The latter we know are reaping huge financial benefits and protections. These three we know support the highly objectionable book "I P N."
> ... L P L has outrageously adopted policies that put youth at the risk to be sick for life or their possible death by allowing books on their shelves that encourage reckless sexual behaviors. The library has chosen this Playboy kind of book for children's entertainment. Youth are their targeted segment of Lewiston's population who have not attained the ability to process without trauma these pornographic illustrations and writings. "I P N" violates youth's period of latency, robs them of their childhood, and greatly infringes upon necessary preparation for responsible adulthood. (Book challenge letter, Lewiston, ME, January 30, 2008)

Note that the challenger describes herself as being "not guilty" on the charge of civil theft. Although her language seems somewhat exaggerated, it is, in fact, typical of challengers' discourse. As will be demonstrated throughout the study, challengers often employ martial language that associates the presence of a book and its availability to children and youth in public institutions as an act of war.

This chapter delineates the themes in challengers' discourse concerning the decline of society, the role of public institutions in the local community, the role of parents in children's lives, and the innocence of childhood. That is, it is concerned with specific social/structural aspects of challengers' worldviews. First, the chapter explores challengers' understanding of society with particular emphasis on the theme of moral decline and its consequences for the health of American society. Second, the chapter looks at challengers' construction of public institutions and the roles that these institutions should play in local communities. Next, the chapter explores the theme of parenthood, especially the role of parents in their children's lives and the relationship between parenting and public institutions. Finally, the chapter discusses challengers' construction of childhood innocence and how objectionable material leads to its loss and corrupts the moral guidance that parents provide for their children.

A SENSE OF MORAL DRIFT IN SOCIETY

The decline of society is one of the most common themes in challengers' discourse. As the Lewiston challenger states, the Lewiston Public Library (along with SIECUS and Planned Parenthood) is out to "destroy our great nation." These organizations are the "enemy" of society for the challenger—enemies that are actively working to put an end to American society as we have known it. The prevalence of this theme throughout challengers' discourse gives us some sense of how book challenges in public institutions draw on, to use Bourdieu's term, the structuring structure of discourse employed in the so-called culture wars. For example, one speaker at a public hearing in Stockton, Missouri, argued against the inclusion of Sherman Alexie's book *The Absolutely True Diary of a Part-Time Indian* in the school's curriculum:

> And all we have seen over the last 50 years is a slide further and further into debauchery and rebellion against righteousness, principles, ethics and morality . . . the parameters by which they chose the book, I didn't see anything in here about values, or morality, or our ability to care for individuals. Moral drift of the society. I am an honest person that is necessarily against this book but I am a person that is for the public having the right to elect officials who make decisions such as you made and I want to thank you for your decision that you made and I support it. And I want to say that I am 100% for the decision you made. (Male speaker #1, Book challenge hearing, Stockton, MO, September 8, 2010)

It is clear from the speaker's statement that society's morals were more in keeping with his own 50 years ago and changes in the guiding morals and principles since then have only been to society's detriment. According to the challenger, the boundaries of permissibility have radically changed over the past 50 years. This has resulted in the values of contemporary society being significantly different from what they were in the recent past. This theme of a moral shift in society is present in the discourse of many challengers. In another example, a challenger from Helena, Montana, echoes this sentiment in a letter to the board. Here the 1960s are identified as when the problems for "our youth" began:

> Many people wonder why our youth are in the trouble they are in today vs. fifty years ago. Well, just take a look at what is being forced down the throats

of our youth today. Allowing this book to be a part of our school's curriculum reflects on the values of the Helena community. (Letter to the board, Helena, MT, December 3, 2010)

This letter writer is also referring to *The Absolutely True Diary of a Part-Time Indian* and it is clear that, for the challenger, the ready availability of this book to young people is a symbol of the moral decline of society. At the same time, the writer implies that 50 years ago, the youth of the country were not "in trouble" because they were not permitted to read such objectionable material. For the Stockton, Missouri, challenger quoted previously, this shift in morals has even affected the standards by which schools choose educational materials. Here one can see the book playing a dual role in challengers' discourse—it is both symbol and symptom of the deterioration of society. The importance of institutions in the discourse of challengers will be discussed in more depth in the next section, but it is important to note here that institutions are considered major participants in the decline of society.

The Stockton challenger also argues that "morality" is no longer a criterion for inclusion in the school's curriculum as it had been in the past. Although this challenger does not explicitly state which morals were present in society in the past and are now in decline, other challengers offer several examples of how morals have changed, including in the areas of sexual mores, explicit violence, and the presence of stereotypes in literature. These changes in sexual mores are discussed in the following request for reconsideration form:

> The theme of this book is an extreme version of a "coming of age" of our current society which has been infiltrated by different forms of media pushing illicit sex, graphic situations, and an ultracasual view of morality. Do we need to join in on the assault of decency? (Request for reconsideration #1, Clarkstown, NY, date redacted [February 2011])

Note that the use of the term "current" here indicates that there was some time in the past when society had a different view of "coming of age." According to this challenger, childhood used to be "decent." Now the media, with the complicity of public institutions, is identified as an infiltrator that pushes new morals, particularly those regarding sexuality, onto society.

Some of these new values that the media pushes are more concrete than others. For example, it is difficult to know what the challenger means by "graphic situations," though in the statement above it seems to be linked to illicit sex. "Morality" per se is never fully defined by this particular challenger, but one can assume that to be moral means not engaging in illicit sex. The statement "ultracasual view of morality" implies a prevailing sense that the media does not sufficiently emphasize possible consequences of such behavior. What these consequences might be is not specified by this particular challenger, but one gets the sense that they are calamitous. There is a feeling that administrators who allow such material in libraries or schools are unaware of the catastrophic consequences to their decisions.

The challenger in Lewiston, Maine, offers a very succinct definition of how society has declined morally. She particularly focuses on gender roles and the protection of children:

> A culture is civilized inasmuch as women and children are respected and defended by men. To the degree that children are respected enough to be given the best possible education in preparation for their human vocation will be the degree of the strength and respect of the United States in the world. One reputable organization has produced what is known the "Map Of Shame." This map indicates the nations in the world that are literally sliding off the face of the earth because these nations are targeting their own people for extinction. "I P N" is just one small but very effective pawn being used to cause our great nation to possibly be one of those nations going the way of the dinosaur and included in this "Map Of Shame." (Book challenge letter, Lewiston, ME, January 30, 2008)

This challenger clearly states that a civilized society can only exist if men and women fulfill traditional gender roles where men are the protectors and women are the protected, and failing to do so means that the United States is no longer a moral nation. Here one can see how the presence of objectionable material in a public institution signifies a greater moral decline—the institution becomes a "small but effective pawn" in the moral drift of society. That is, both the book (a symptom) and its presence on the shelves of the local public library (a symbol) are constructed as both an object and an action that signifies that the nation is in decline. The Lewiston Public Library, in its failure to fulfill its prescribed role as defender, is no longer playing a civilizing role in society when it allows a book like *It's Perfectly Normal* on its shelves. This is directly related to the construction of public institutions in challengers' discourse as places that must share the larger community's values.

This sense of decline in society and—following from this—in local institutions also appeared in an interview I had with one of the Helena, Montana, challengers, who noted that "our culture has gotten away from a standard. And we don't follow a standard anymore as to how to live. How to treat one another. And that's just had a huge effect" (Interview with challenger, Helena, MT, December 12, 2011). One of the standards in this and other testimony from challengers refers to the standards of selection used by public libraries in the schools. As noted above, at some point in the past, books like the ones in question would never have been allowed on library shelves or in school curricula in the first place. Their presence as a signifier of a greater change and part of an active attack on the "standards" of the past is implied in such statements. For challengers, society is more than just a collection of people in a given geographic space—society, discussed here as "the nation" or the "community" or just "we," is the backbone for living a moral life. Throughout their discourse, challengers are concerned with the values and morals that are condoned by society and argue that without a strong backbone, society will collapse. If poor values are acceptable in the larger society, then the world as it is known today is doomed. It is important to note that this is not a wholly nostalgic argument. Instead, it is more accurate to view it as a reactionary argument. As discussed in the previous chapter, challenges can be seen as a reaction to both social and demographic changes in society. The challengers do not necessarily want to fully return to the past (although it is possible that some do) but instead they are more concerned with what will happen if society continues on its current trajectory.

Challengers argue that public institutions are essential partners in stemming the moral decline of society within a local community. They construct public institutions as more than simply depositories—they are public symbols of the community itself and should also be spaces of both safety and orderly knowledge. In fact, these two traits are often mutually dependent for challengers: if difficult, unsanctioned knowledge is present in a school curriculum or public library collections, then the institution cannot be considered a safe, trustworthy place.[2] This is true regardless of the physical safety of patrons and students within the institutions.

CONTROVERSIES IN PUBLIC INSTITUTIONS

The term "public institutions" is used here to collectively designate public libraries and public schools. These are institutions that are supported by the public through taxes and it is this economic support that unifies the two institutions throughout the study as sites of study. Of primary importance for this study is that these are public institutions within the public sphere. Public sphere is defined here as the social space that is created by the reflexive circulation of discourse. Although "public" is defined as an institution that is "supported by the community," it must be noted, however, that "publics" are also a more abstract concept that operate, as Michael Warner states, as a "social totality."[3] Warner defines a public as a relationship among strangers that *must* consist of strangers. Publics in this sense are self-organizing and, in modern capitalist society, often only exist because of the powerlessness of the individual. They also exist as a social space created through the circulation of discourse. Administrators and staff of these public institutions deliberately choose materials that become part of the public discourse within the public sphere. For challengers, public institutions are also sites of control and power where their economic capital is transformed into symbolic capital.

This section explores several different themes concerning public institutions in challengers' discourse including how they construct both public and school libraries and the role of controversial books in public school curricula.

What Is a Library?

Libraries fulfill many institutional roles for challengers but, in general, they are defined as institutions that lend many different types of materials to patrons of all ages. They are also seen as places of refuge and safety within the local community. Challengers also structure libraries, especially public libraries, as institutions that embody the First Amendment of the United States Constitution—that is, they are a physical embodiment of free speech. The availability of a book in the local public library means that the book is available to all. For example, in a school curriculum challenge, the existence of public libraries in a community is sometimes used as a justification for removing a book from the curriculum. In Clarkstown, New York, challengers were attempting to remove the book from both the English curriculum and school libraries. The following challenger argues that because the book is available in public libraries, she and her fellow challengers are not engaging in censorship:

> And all have one thing available to us, it's called libraries so to ask for a book not to be promoted in our school doesn't mean that we're censoring it, it just means that we would like for it not to be the curriculum for our child. Not to say that all of our children might not go to the library and take it out. But that's their choice and that's the choice between the parent and the child and something that they can discuss. (Female speaker #6, Book challenge hearing, Clarkstown, NY, March 24, 2011)

In this instance the public library becomes a kind of "cover" for the challenge. If the book is available in the library, then removing it from the curriculum is not banning the book. For this challenger, libraries are seen as a venue for collecting all knowledge while the school curriculum should be reserved for ideas that she deems legitimate. In this instance, public libraries are the only spaces in which censorship can take place.

On the other hand, some challengers see the school library as an embodiment of the First Amendment within a public educational institution. For example, the following speaker, a member of the Merrill (Wisconsin) School Board, notes that removing the book from the school library would be unconstitutional. Immediately prior to this statement, the speaker explained his vote to remove the book from the school curriculum:

> No on the library part, I feel . . . obviously on the First Amendment that we . . . our founding fathers were light years ahead of their time when they developed

these amendments for us. I feel that one thing I would like to see changed would be if there is an individual parent that does not want their child to read a certain book with the system that we have in place. Let them know that they could call the district or the school to have that book on list and then they can't check them out. At that time the district is still [supporting] the First Amendment and we are not in any way denying any rights. You still have the authority as the parent. (Male speaker #6, Book challenge hearing, Merrill, WI, September 29, 2011)

Although it is not stated explicitly, the speaker seems to be arguing that removing the book from the school library would be infringing on students' First Amendment rights.[4] However, this is coupled with the idea that parents' authority trumps a student's wish to read the book. The board member argues that the district would still be upholding the First Amendment if a parent calls and requests that his or her child not be able to check out a particular book.[5] The theme of parents as boundary setters vis-à-vis their children's consumption of media will be discussed in more detail in the next section of this chapter.

Schools, per se, were rarely discussed in challengers' discourse. However, it is implicit in many of their arguments that schools should also be places of safety for children. One challenger described how the school library is part of the overall educational mission of the school and therefore has a different purpose from the public library, while other challengers do not make any distinction between a school and public library:

Looking at it from a school's perspective I know that the school library is vastly different than a regular public library. They both have different rules, policies, regulations, and morals. A school library serves only students. One main rule of a school library and a school board is to protect students. If the content were put into a movie we teachers could not show that content in our classrooms. If it was on a website, it would be blocked by our server. (Male speaker #8, Book challenge hearing, Stockton, MO, September 8, 2010)

For this challenger, the idea of protection for students is offered as a justification for removing a book from the school library. Precisely because it is not a public library, administrators will not be acting unconstitutionally if the book is removed. As part of the school, the school library is structured as a space that should instead ensure students' safety. One aspect of school challenges that make them somewhat different from public library challenges is the issue of coercion. Challengers often take issue with the idea that their children are required to read books with which they disagree.

Controversial Books in the Curriculum

Challenges to materials in schools are often quite complex as the particular book in question might be challenged on the basis of its inclusion in the required curriculum, recommended book lists, and/or school library collections. Sometimes challengers request that objectionable materials be removed from all three sections of the institution while other challenges are solely against the books' presence in the curriculum or in the school media center. The idea that removing books from the curriculum is not unconstitutional is clearly stated by the following writer. Although primarily an argument concerning the ability of non–Native American teachers to conduct a discussion of the book *Brave New World*, the writer also argues that the book should remain in the school library:

> I was told that the argument against removing the text was based on first amendment rights. This is an invalid argument because our request is to remove the text from the required reading list assigned and taught by primarily non-Native SPS [Seattle Public Schools] teachers. I believe this book should remain in the library and as a summer reading option. The primary issue which is pertinent to this meeting today, is that this book is required reading and that the SPS teaching staff lacks the insight, knowledge base and accurate information to successfully balance classroom discussions. In addition, there is no mandated or required lesson plan to adequately, respectfully address the racist content of this text. (Letter to the board, Seattle, WA, August 23, 2010)

The letter writer's concern is focused on the presence of the book in the curriculum. She takes an interesting position wherein the writer is concerned that adequate discussion of the book will not be possible in the classroom but the book should still be available "in the library and as a summer reading option." That is, the curriculum is structured as a space of orderly knowledge while the school library is a place of more freedom. Since children are required to read materials in the curriculum, these materials must fit within particular categories of knowledge. For this challenger, the library and summer reading lists are spaces where what she classifies as difficult or forbidden knowledge can be made available for students. Students should never be *required* to be exposed to such knowledge. If such information is made available, it leads to the challengers losing trust in the teachers and administrators of schools.

In almost all cases, and as was discussed in chapter 1, challengers discuss their loss of trust in the school system and their fear that their children will be coerced into being exposed to morals with which they disagree. For example, in the following testimony by a parent in Westfield, New Jersey, the challenger notes that she has lost trust in the school system since the institution was not clear in describing the procedures by which the book in question,

Alexie's *Absolutely True Diary of a Part-Time Indian*, was chosen for inclusion in the freshman English class:

> I still feel that I'm not completely in trust of the system and I really would like to regain that trust. And I would like to work together to address this problem to prevent it from happening again in the future. Westfield has always been one of the top schools in our state and that is due [to] its exceptional teachers and students. We are recognizing this by highlighting the point that this was not customary for Westfield. This is atypical. It's an aberration to what typically happens here. I have already made my concerns known with this book. But I still feel we have crossed a new line. It may not be this book that you're concerned with but it could be a book in the future of which you may not approve. (Female speaker #5, Book challenge hearing, Westfield, NJ, February 28, 2012)

Note that the challenger describes the inclusion of the book as a "line that has been crossed" with respect to the administration of the public schools. Prior to her discovery of the book's inclusion, she trusted the administration to provide materials for the children of her community that were in keeping with her own ideas of what is appropriate. The presence of the objectionable book, operating as a symbol, has caused her to mistrust the institution. She also warns other parents that their own trust in the system is misplaced.

According to challengers, public libraries and schools have a duty to protect children and aid parents in their roles as boundary setters. Within these institutions, children should be free to move around without encountering objectionable material. One of the interviewees noted this idea of safety when discussing taking the children she cared for to the local public library: "We would go to the library and get books or videos or things. Whatnot. I would go to the children's area which is set aside and feel like the kids could get whatever book from that section" (Interview with challenger, Carrollton, TX, January 3, 2012). For this challenger, the library is constructed as a safe place where the children could check out whatever they wanted from the children's section. The collections themselves, and not just the perceived physical safety of the building, made the library a safe place for the challenger. If the institution fails to do so, then they fail to help parents protect their children.

FAMILY AND PARENTING

It is difficult to overstate the importance of parenting in the discourse of challengers. For many challengers, parenting is more than just a simple role—it is constructed as a job that one has willingly assumed, and, like other jobs, it requires time, skill, and specialized knowledge. Throughout their discourse, challengers focus on several important aspects of the role of parenting. These ideas are well represented in the following testimony from a challenger in Westfield, New Jersey:

> The key is about parents having the ability to have their rights respected. About what their children are exposed to. And if a lot of parents have no problem with what they're exposed to that's fine. Let them do it. That's why the book has to be made optional for parents who are unhappy with their children being exposed to it. (Male speaker #1, Book challenge hearing, Westfield, NJ, February 28, 2012)

First, parents must set boundaries and maintain a certain amount of control over their children's lives. Second, coupled with the idea that even though it is the parents' job to set limits for their children, many parents do not, and they are—essentially—falling down on the job. Finally, there is the sense that parenting is difficult and that public institutions must help parents with the difficult task of raising children. For challengers the meaning of parenting and the role of parents in children and youth's lives is often described as one of authority and power. They often draw on discourse from the realm of economics and their arguments are imbued with an undercurrent of anxiety concerning the work of others who fulfill the role.

Boundary Setting

Parents, of course, have many different roles to play in their children's lives. For many challengers, one of the most important is that of boundary setter. Parents must set restrictions for their children's behavior and impose punishments when they go outside of these limits. As will be discussed in the next section, children are often constructed in challengers' discourse as innocent vessels who, through education and life experiences, are filled with knowledge from various sources. One of parents' most important roles is to protect this innocence by setting boundaries. An important source for knowledge, especially moral knowledge, comes from children's own awareness of the boundaries that are set by their parents regarding moral behavior. For example, in Westfield, New Jersey, one of the challengers clearly describes this role of parents vis-à-vis the role of schools:

> Pretty radical stuff today. The concept of parents not having any involvement in the education of their children. Leaving it all up to the teachers. That is crazy, nutty stuff. I mean it's our children. It's the children we're talking about and they're consumers and we're the taxpayers of it. That's some crazy stuff man. . . .
>
> But parents have a right to not want to subject their children to those sentiments in the ninth grade. That right has to be respected and you guys are like we hear ya, we heard about it, but we're going to compromise. (Male speaker #1, Book challenge hearing, Westfield, NJ, February 28, 2012)

This challenger is particularly adamant about the role of parents in their children's moral development. Also note that the speaker draws on the larger discourse of parents' rights in his argument. This discourse focuses on the rights of parents to have absolute control over their children's moral development. For many challengers, setting moral limits is both a parent's right vis-à-vis the board of education and constitutes his or her proper role in the family structure and is connected to larger ideas of liberty in American society. The following speaker in Bedford, New Hampshire, also describes this role using somewhat less aggressive language than the previous challenger:

> For people who want this book, they can ask for it, the book is available. Go buy it. Get it online. I didn't let my kids when they were five watch R-rated movies for the same reasons. You need to draw a line as to what is appropriate and what's not. If other parents want to provide other information to their kids. Fine. It's up to them. But I don't think we need to have it in the public schools. (Male speaker #5, Book challenge hearing, Bedford, NH, February 28, 2011)

Here the challenger argues that other parents can simply get the book from another source while at the same time scolding parents for being willing to provide such objectionable material to their children.

The idea of "drawing lines" for children regarding the media that they consume is also a common theme throughout challengers' discourse. Some media are considered inappropriate and it is the duty and responsibility of parents to make sure that their children are not exposed to problematic movies, books, or television. Note that the speaker in Bedford points to institutionalized film ratings as an aid for setting boundaries for children. Although this use of labeling will be discussed in more detail in chapter 6, a brief discussion of how challengers construct ratings is warranted here. The film ratings are both a structuring and structured structure: when a film is given an R rating it is perceived as a certain type of film—one that is not appropriate for the challengers' children. To the challenger the book in question is analogous to an R-rated film (though one without the structuring device of ratings) and therefore should not be made available to students. That is, the book is structured as being inappropriate for children. It is interesting that the challenge concerns a book in the high school curriculum and he uses the age of five in his analogy. However, this seems to be a rhetorical device within the discourse of censorship to indicate just how inappropriate the challenged book is for students. That is, the book is so objectionable it is comparable to showing an R-rated movie to a five-year-old child.

Many challengers tend to see boundaries as part of a framework for inculcating values and morals in children. By setting limits, parents demonstrate moral right and wrong for their children. For the challenger below, the boundaries are themselves values (prior to this challenger's testimony, several students had also expressed their positions concerning the challenge case at the hearing in Clarkstown, New York):

> So first of all, I am impressed by the students here. I think it's a good thing but everybody also needs to remember that what you teach your children at home, whether it's books or whether it's TV, everybody has to be aware that that's your foundation. If you're strict at home with your children, the educators should support that. And I know that there's problems. I know that six and seventh graders back in 1992 were talking about sex and parents their parents apparatuses in the classroom. Now if you want to talk about keeping in line with good morals and values that's fine everybody deserves the opportunity to read or not read. And so everybody should be respectful of everyone else. (Female speaker #5, Book challenge hearing, Clarkstown, NY, March 24, 2011)

The challenger is clear that it is the role of parents to set boundaries for their children in the home. Interestingly, media is understood to be an important aspect of being "taught" proper morals and values. It exists as part of an educational framework and forms a foundation for the moral development of children. Although there might be problems throughout the school system, the institution should still support the efforts of "strict" parents.

Boundary setting is constructed by many challengers as a commonsense skill for parents. Although, as will be discussed below, parenting can be difficult, establishing boundaries is one of the most basic actions any parent can perform. As one challenger in Clarkstown, New York, states, "Now, look, read the book and then see if this is appropriate for your son or daughter. You don't have to have the tools to teach your son or daughter this correctly—go out on the streets and get it" (Male speaker #6, Book challenge hearing, Clarkstown, NY, March 24, 2011). The skills that one needs for parenting are available "on the street" and it is one's duty as a parent to develop these skills. According to the challenger applying this knowledge, it will be obvious that the book in question is not appropriate.

The question of appropriateness is a charged one for challengers, as the presence or absence of appropriate material determines the safety of a public institution. One of the interviewees states that going through the challenge helped her clarify what was appropriate for her children to read and how to steer her children toward such material:

> The book's still there and I have three more children that will be in that building. They know . . . we've now had lots of talks about what's appropriate to pick out and what's not. This gives [us] a chance to set some boundaries as far as what they're allowed to read because I hadn't even thought that there would be a book like that in the library. To be a selection as a possibility. Now I think a little differently. (Interview with challenger, Central York, PA, December 7, 2011)

Even with these limits in place and her own personal awareness of the different kinds of books available in the school library, the challenger is still concerned that her children will encounter objectionable material. Note that she is somewhat surprised that the book was available to children in the first place and is concerned that, even with the limits she has placed on her children's media consumption, they will still come into contact with media of which she disapproves. The experience of the challenge taught her that her values do not necessarily align with the school's, and this has made her somewhat wary of the institution as a whole.

The theme of boundary setting also introduces the subject of control over children's moral development into challengers' discourse. The following challenger from Westfield, New Jersey, argues that she and her fellow challengers are looking for respect from both other parents and the schools:

> Our requests are very reasonable and we really just want more transparency. Anyone may pick up this book and read it if they choose to on their own volition. I am in no way imposing my beliefs on anyone nor am I suggesting that they are superior to anyone else's, I'm simply asking that others respect those beliefs that are shared by so many in this country. I am not the one making a controversial book a requirement in school nor am I taking it away. We respectfully did not highlight the mishandling in the paper or anywhere else in the hope that this could be resolved in an efficient way. (Female speaker #5, Book challenge hearing, Westfield, NJ, February 28, 2012)

As noted throughout this study, parents are often concerned with the idea that certain books are required reading. One possible remedy that they offer is to simply make the books an optional part of the curriculum. (Although note that there are also challenges against books that are on recommended book lists.) This is a method of maintaining power over their children's education in public schools. It is important to note that this is only needed for particular books and it also, in some respects, lessens the authority of teachers and other educators and their own power over the school curriculum.

Although public schools and libraries should help parents set boundaries, for challengers, it is parents who have ultimate authority over the moral development of their children:

> My responsibility as a parent supersedes that of a teacher or any national interest group. I am the most qualified person to tell the board what is appropriate for my child. No board, community group will ultimately answer for the content of my child's education or the content of their integrity. That is my responsibility. It is the responsibility of this board, in my opinion, to represent the will and values of this community that elected them to this position of public trust. (Male speaker #6, Book challenge hearing, Stockton, MO, September 8, 2010)

Parents not only decide what is appropriate for their children, their decision making is a reflection of themselves to the wider society. If their children do not have "integrity," then they have failed as parents. "Parent" is constructed by parents as not simply a role but as having great social meaning, and one's achievements as a parent will be evaluated by others in society. Parents are especially important when it comes to deciding when their children should be exposed to difficult knowledge. For challengers, such an important task should never be in the power of strangers. This idea that parents have ultimate control leads directly to the next theme regarding the failure of other parents to do their jobs correctly. If parents are the ultimate arbiters of moral development for their children, what does it mean when they fail to do so?

"Other Parents"

"Other parents," writ large, are of great concern to many challengers and a common theme throughout their discourse is that other parents are "falling down on the job." The implication here is that "I am a good parent but those parents are not." As one of the speakers at the public hearing in Merrill, Wisconsin, states, "Some parents—I don't want to say that they don't care but they don't have the time or resources to read every book that the school puts forth to our kids" (Female speaker #7, Book challenge hearing, Merrill, WI, September 29, 2011). This speaker implies that it is part of parents' job to read all the books assigned to their children but some parents simply do not have the resources to do so. Another challenger states:

> It sounds pretty conservative, I know, but I think it has a lot to do [with] the lack of parental involvement in what their kids are reading. The themes. A lot of children around here are allowed to play video games or allowed games of a violent nature. We certainly don't allow those in our house. Not something we encourage or permit them to do while other children their age are allowed to play graphic video games and read whatever literature they want. I don't know if it's lack of parental involvement or they just think it's not damaging or I'm not sure why that it is. (Interview with challenger, Central York, PA, December 7, 2011)

The interviewee's statement implies that she is concerned with the moral development of both her own and other people's children. Other parents do not seem to understand the damage they are inflicting on their children when they allow them to read violent material. As shown in the illustration described in Stephen Colclough's *Consuming Texts* where an Industrial Age father is unaware of the salacious books his daughters are investigating, these parents are either ignorant or neglectful.[6]

This theme of differing standards of parenting is quite common in challengers' discourse. "Other parents" are simply teaching their children incivility in the eyes of many challengers. Another interviewee states:

> We thought . . . we're very involved in our children's lives and what they see, what they watch, what they hear, what they read, and we thought that that's just a testimony to our loving involvement in our children's lives. And I know it's not that way with a lot of children in our schools today. The rudeness. The crassness. The vulgarity. That difference, I believe, is a testimony to how we're involved in our children's lives. (Interview with challenger, Helena, MT, December 12, 2011)

She is clearly aware of how her parenting differs from others whom she perceives to be less involved in their children's lives than she and her husband are. Other children are more "rude, crass, and vulgar" than her own, and this poor behavior is a direct outcome of their parents' neglect. Similarly, a letter writer from Merrill, Wisconsin, is blunt in her characterization of parents who "fall down on the job." They are simply unaware of the harm they are causing their children:

> I realize that some parents do not care what their kids see or read. I also submit that they are either ignorant of the facts, effect and repercussions of such books or are, in my case, afraid to say anything to the education professionals. They also do not have the time to read all of the books their kids read at school to make an educated decision about what they would like their kid to experience or not experience. I realize that you cannot cater to every parent's wishes, but as a whole would it not be wiser to stay away from such forms of literature? (Letter to the board, Merrill, WI, June 10, 2011)

It is the school's responsibility to not aid these other parents in harming their children. For this challenger, since the other parents do not know the materials their children are reading, schools should eschew adding controversial books in the curriculum. Because other parents are not living up to their role as boundary setters, school and library administrators must help those parents who do not have the time or inclination to impose boundaries and limits on their children.

Institutional Support for Parenting

The idea that parents are busy is a common theme throughout challengers' discourse. As one speaker at the Clarkstown, New York, hearing noted, "We as parents work. We don't have time to read every single material that our kids are viewing" (Female speaker #8, Book challenge hearing, Clarkstown, NY, March 24, 2011). Instead, parents rely on elected representatives to ensure that their own interests are included in library and school policies. The speaker continues: "We vote on you as our representatives and we want you to represent us and to give us the opportunity to depend . . . depend upon you to use good judgment on what you are putting in the curriculum. That's all . . . it is up to you to understand and represent us as parents." Parents, especially those who lack resources, are indebted to administrators and elected officials to make good decisions regarding curriculum and collection materials. The schools and libraries are structured in this discourse as a support system for parents.

Another challenger is concerned that if parents do not receive this support from administrators there will be a rift between parents and their children:

> But I think about kids who have spoken for it and what if they happen to have conservative parents who said "We don't want you to read that book." Then what would that develop between the parent and the child. That causes some kind of division between the parent and child because that child might feel like they're an outsider and you in high school they're all challenging what they've been raised in. Moral values. Religious values. That's what they're all going through. So they don't need a book presented by the school to add to that. (Female speaker #5, Book challenge hearing, Clarkstown, NY, March 24, 2011)

Once again there is fear that the institution's values do not match the parents'. When this happens, children will feel like outsiders in the school environment. Presumably other children would know that they were not allowed to read a particular book and this would make these children "different" from the others in school. When such a situation occurs, it can cause tension at home.

When public libraries and schools have objectionable material, they make parents' jobs more difficult. According to challengers, administrators of these two institutions have two roles to play. First, they must keep parents informed of what is going on in their institutions. Second, they must ensure that such controversial materials are not available for students. These ideas will be discussed in more detail in the following chapter, but it is important to note that this is how challengers conceptualize the relationship between public institutions and parenting. The following speaker at a hearing in Clarkstown, New York, states these ideas explicitly:

> So, your job is to educate our children and to inform the parents properly so they can make the right decisions as to whether or not what their child is learning squares with their moral values. That was not done. And this is not the first instance. Your job is not to make our job as parents harder. Your job is to help us so that we can develop our children into model young men and women who go out into the world. We are all very busy in this society and I just want to say to all the parents here: take the time and know what your children are

learning. (Male speaker #4, Book challenge hearing, Clarkstown, NY, March 24, 2011)

While the role of the parent is to set boundaries, here it is the role of the school system to help parents enforce these limits. However, the speaker still emphasizes that other parents should be informed of what is happening in their children's lives.

One of the most interesting aspects of the idea that parents must set boundaries—and public institutions must aid them in doing so—is the implicit understanding of children that comes out of this discourse. Children are structured as vessels who are either "filled with ideas" as they grow or individuals who have certain innate traits that are "activated" through exposure to media. As one challenger states:

> We don't want to question the teachers' authority or the educational values that they bring forward. But we do want to be heard. We do want cooperation. We do want to know that you understand that we do understand what our kids are up to. Rules need to be drawn and we need to put in all the good stuff while we can before we let the rest of the world fill them up. Part of it's about society and culture and the culture that we build in our school systems in the day to day contact between kids and the adults that they're in contact with. (Female speaker #7, Book challenge hearing, Merrill, WI, September 29, 2011)

Although this quotation is focused on schools, as we have seen above, public libraries are also called on to provide more diffuse support for parents. Here schools are called on to be transparent and cooperative in raising children in the community and also in maintaining their innocence. For many challengers, children are seen as vessels that are slowly filled with knowledge and it is up to parents (with the help of public institutions) to ensure that any knowledge they receive enhances their moral development.

CHILDREN AND INNOCENCE

One of the more intriguing aspects of many challengers' worldviews concerns their construction of children's innocence, as this term is ubiquitous within their discourse. Children are seen as beings in need of protection from the outside world, especially when it comes to protecting their "innocence." Innocence is defined by challengers as a state of unawareness. Children are innocent because they are unaware and uninformed of the world around them unless it is introduced to them.[7] This is, of course, a familiar argument to anyone who is aware of research on the social construction of childhood. However, it is important to note that within challengers' discourse there are two prominent constructions of childhood innocence. The first views the child as a tabula rasa and sees sexuality, violence, vulgarity, and other behaviors as *learned* behaviors. The second construction views childhood as time when these behaviors are *latent*. Sexuality, violence, and vulgarity are already part of a child's natural being but they are only triggered through some outside mechanism. Regardless of the construction that is employed, the action of the challenger is the same: since they lack the requisite interpretive strategies for the material, children must be protected from learning about such behaviors for as long as possible.

The innocence of children, regardless of how it is constructed, is taken as a given for many challengers. It is something that never needs to be explained or discussed, only protected. As one challenger states, "This book is not suitable for children in Elementary school and if I have to start petitions I will then all the parents will see that Westside Elementary committee does not care about the innocence of our children" (Request for reconsideration, Spring Hill, FL, November 10, 2010). For challengers, there is a direct relationship between not supporting the challengers' position and being unwilling to protect children. To disagree with the challengers' assessment of a particular book means that one is unconcerned with children's innocence.

Children's need for protection is a primary justification throughout requests for reconsideration of collection or curriculum materials. The following letter writer from Stockton, Missouri, discusses how this is one of the primary duties of the local school board: "We are certainly blessed to have a School Board that will stand in protection of our children and young people and not be bent by vocal critics" (Letter to the board, Stockton, MO, May 13, 2010). This need for protection is evident in another speaker's testimony regarding challenged material in Helena, MT, where the book is compared to manure:

> Our children do not need to roll in bad things to understand their nature. But there is an interesting phenomenon about manure. If one works near it for enough time, it begins to lose its smell, and one is less concerned with getting away. How can it be wise to go out of our way to expose children and teenagers to what is in essence—manure? It defies common sense. (Female speaker #2, Book challenge hearing, Helena, MT, December 2, 2010)

For this challenger, part of the maturation process is learning how to understand one's own nature and being able to recognize the difference between good and bad behaviors. The challenger holds the tabula rasa view of childhood: if children are exposed to the objectionable material, they will no longer recognize why it is problematic and it will instead become part of their overall character. As children are filled with knowledge, they slowly become a particular type of person with agency and personality and it is vital that administrators of public institutions do their part to ensure that they are on the correct path. Also note the challenger's use of the term "manure."

The following commenter at a public hearing clearly explains that it is also the duty of parents to protect children from problematic material. Prior to this comment, she described Jiminy Cricket from Walt Disney's *Pinocchio* as an exemplar of positive values in media:

> Esteemed board members, I've witnessed the values of power and control supersede the values of purity and integrity and goodness during the debate over *Montana 1948*. And the power and control of issues do not rest with the parents. We are here to defend our children from obscenity and corruption. For me it is a shame to find safety and virtue in Walt Disney but not in the representatives of my community. Thank you. (Female speaker #7, Book challenge hearing, Merrill, WI, September 29, 2011)

As found in discourse throughout this study, the language used is martial. This challenger notes that parents must "defend" children from outside forces that are filled with definite dangers to children since these forces are filled with "obscenity and corruption." Another writer also uses the martial language of spiritual warfare to describe the effect of a permissive society on childhood innocence:

> The world assaults our children every day with profane and obscene use through countless outlets. Why do some feel the need to perpetuate that assault in the guise of preparing our children for the real world? Why do we recognize that the material is vulgar yet feel the need to expose our children to it? (Male speaker #6, Book challenge hearing, Stockton, MO, September 8, 2010)

For this challenger, profanity and obscenity are so prevalent throughout society that parents must stand with the school board in vigilance. If they do not, children will be harmed risking both health and life and failing to become responsible adults. The challenger in Lewiston, Maine, writes:

> L P L has outrageously adopted policies that put youth at the risk to be sick for life or their possible death by allowing books on their shelves that encourage reckless sexual behaviors. The library has chosen this Playboy kind of book for children's entertainment. Youth are their targeted segment of Lewiston's population who have not attained the ability to process without trauma these pornographic illustrations and writings. "I P N" violates youth's period of latency, robs them of their childhood, and greatly infringes upon necessary preparation for responsible adulthood. (Letter to the board, Lewiston, ME, January 30, 2008)

The challenger in Lewiston makes an explicit link between the challenged material and risks to children's health. Note that this challenger uses the second construction of childhood innocence wherein youth is a "period of latency." If children encounter objectionable material, then they will be aware of their own potential to be, for example, "sexually reckless." Presumably for this challenger, children's sexuality is unrealized until they are either told about it by outsiders or it is awakened through reading. She also argues that the book contains knowledge that will have extremely dire effects from which the children will not be able to recover. The idea that reading can have profound effects on the development of children is explored more in the following chapter. For now, it is clear that challengers argue that adults must protect children from the perceived harm that will come from reading the challenged materials. As the following writer states, it is up to administrators to ensure that children are protected: "We approve the school board's action for the book Absolutely True Diary of a Part-Time Indian. Thank you for making this stand and for your part in protecting our children's mind [*sic*]" (Letter to the board, Stockton, MO, May 10, 2010). The issue of protecting children is ubiquitous in the discourse of challengers. For many of them, this is why they challenged a particular book in the first place—to safeguard the minds of the innocent.

One of the interviewees is explicit in her assessment of what inappropriate material does to children:

> There can be a story written about, a mystery that doesn't involve violence. So for me it's just a little about taking away that childhood innocence when you . . . you know expose them to that kind of violent imagery you can never get that out of your head. So I just thought it was not appropriate for children as young as 8 years old, for that to be in that library. (Interview with challenger, Central York, PA, December 7, 2011)

This is the tabula rasa view of childhood: children's minds did not contain objectionable knowledge before it was introduced and once there it cannot be removed. Children who consume the objectionable material will no longer be innocent. As introduced in chapter 2, children are constructed as having an undisciplined imagination and are therefore unable to have critical distance from a text. This concept is discussed in more detail in chapter 5.

Another challenger also presents the idea that once certain ideas are introduced to children, they cannot be erased:

> Finally the tragedy that scores of minors are having their minds warped and corrupted by images and themes they'll remember for the rest of their lives. Images and themes that scintillate and seduce. Images and themes they are entirely unqualified and unprepared to handle or process. (Request for reconsideration #1, Clarkstown, NY, date redacted [February 2011])

The objectionable material leads to the corruption of innocence. Since the children are innocent, either as a tabula rasa or existing within a latent period, they simply do not have the mental capacity to handle the information given in the challenged book. For challengers, the effects of such material cannot be underestimated:

> Hearing teachers and admins defend this book is alarming especially after hearing how children had to disclose how their innocence had been stolen from them in real life. If the nature of public education is to scandalize and sexualize our children, then my children will have no part in the public school system. Our children are victimized enough outside of school: from the promotion of underage sex to the idolization of anorexic pop stars to the marketing of destructive hormonal pills. Our beautiful children have been come instruments for profit and for social engineering and experimentation. I dare say that includes our school district. (Female speaker #7, Book challenge hearing, Merrill, WI, September 29, 2011)

Through exposure to the challenged material, children become victims of a larger system that attempts to exploit them. Because they are innocents that are filled with knowledge through the education process, children are in need of protection from institutions such as public schools. It is clear from the statement above that this particular challenger has lost faith in the ability of this public institution to protect the innocence of children in her community. These public institutions have become the same as the rest of society—organizations that victimize children.

CONCENTRIC CIRCLES OF DECLINE

It is clear from the arguments in this chapter that challenges to materials in public institutions are filled with passion. Individuals feel strongly about the challenged material and are often willing to engage in a type of public advocacy that is novel to them. The testimony and written statements given throughout challenge cases often swing wildly from a discussion of the challenged material to a defense of life and liberty. Even though the challengers in this study are from all over the United States and, in many cases, challenging different books, there are several themes that are common throughout their justifications for removing a book from a school's curriculum or a public library's shelves. These justifications reveal some of the structures that make up the worldviews, or road maps for action, of these challengers.

As noted throughout this study, the themes discussed in this chapter do not constitute complete worldviews but do disclose some of the structures for cognition and meaning that challengers use when arguing for the removal or relocation of a particular book. As discussed in chapters 1 and 2, the discourse that challengers use is understood as a type of poetic wherein individuals work within an institutionalized structure when developing arguments for a particular point of view. Poetics is defined here as the creative practices of individuals that take place within a structured space—it is how one uses the repertoires available for justifying one's actions. Some of these repertoires include discourses employed in other spheres, including education and politics. In Bourdieu's terms, the poetic takes place within an individual's habitus—between and among structuring structures and structured structures. In some respects, these various aspects of society operate as concentric circles of influence with society itself in the larger, outer circle and children in the smaller, innermost circle. Each of these circles exerts power over the next circle with society exerting authority over community, which has power over local institutions, which in turn exerts power over parents, who have authority over their children. Challengers see these circles of spheres as having immense influence over the moral development of both their own and other community members' children. In light of this, it is imperative that media available in local, public institutions be a solely positive force in children's lives.

Society—A Fragile Backbone

Challengers view society as a backbone of life that should provide "good" morals and values to its members. Drawing on the discourse of the culture wars, they see the society of thirty to fifty years ago as one that provided "good morals" for its citizens. Since then American society has shifted profoundly and, in some respects, the fragility of a previous moral consensus has been revealed. This is the essence of the argument regarding moral drift discussed above. The 1960s, in particular, was a time of upheaval throughout American society, and the nation is just beginning to see the outcomes of that shift. This is a well-known argument throughout political discourse in the United States concerning those of a conservative mind-set on the red, right hand of the political spectrum and those of a more liberal mind-set on the blue left. For the purposes of this study, even though the challengers are political actors, it is more fruitful to explore their arguments using sociotheoretical frameworks that focus on symbolic power since, in a time of ubiquitous access, their actions are largely symbolic. These frameworks from outside the political realm provide a more nuanced understanding of their justifications.

The challengers' justifications are based on more than a simple political framework. Instead they see shifts in the actual structures that shape their worldviews. Moral drift is not simply a political moral drift but a change to the structures of civilization as it has been known. Alterations in sexual mores, changes in gender roles, the ubiquity of violence, and the prevalence of obscenity all point to a shift in structure of culture and society. For the challengers, it is the structuring structures of society that have shifted. What is recognized as "society" has been altered over the past 50 years. The meaning of these shifts, that is, their structured structures, is profound, as it indicates for the challengers a change in the very fabric of civilization. This analysis may seem exaggerated, but it is clear from the challengers' discourse that they view these moral shifts in somewhat apocalyptic terms especially with regard to the consequences of these shifts on society. There is an ongoing assault on what they view as moral and, as will be shown in chapter 6, they are the embattled. This viewpoint helps to explain some of the language used throughout challengers' testimony. As stated above, the objectionable material both signifies and is a symptom of society's moral decline.

Public Institutions

For challengers, public libraries and schools are more than just buildings—they are public symbols of the community whose staff, in their role as proxies for the community, must both choose collection materials that consist of legitimate knowledge, and by choosing certain materials, legitimize that knowledge. These institutions operate as both structuring structures and structured structures. As structuring structures, "libraries" and "schools" are perceived as an outward symbol of the community, and therefore the presence of certain materials in curricula and collections *means* that the community also considers these materials to be legitimate knowledge. It is their work as a structured structure within the challengers' symbolic universe that is of primary importance here. As discussed in chapter 2, symbolic capital is a concealed form of economic capital that relates to concepts of prestige and authority in society. This means that public institutions operate as a site of power for challengers. The presence of a public library in a community also conveys a certain status where the economic capital of the community is transformed into a library for everyone in the community.

Because the institutions are paid for by tax money from the community, challengers argue that public libraries and schools should—in all ways—represent the values of the community. The collections and curricula contain knowledge that is sanctioned by the entire community since it is paid for by members of the community. When objectionable materials are found on the shelves or in curricula, challengers argue that the institution is no longer symbolically representing the community in the best light to the rest of society. Within the worldview of challengers, only through the removal, relocation, or restriction of the offending material can the positive symbolic capital of the institution be restored. The public library and school are also vital parts of the local community for challengers. They both represent the community to the wider world and also shape the values and morals of the next generation. Public libraries, in particular, are seen as embodiments of the First Amendment of the U.S. Constitution. As symbolic objects, community-supported public institutions provide a particular image of the community to the wider society and it is this, as well as the sense that these institutions must be a place of safety, that so concerns challengers.

Throughout their discourse, challengers argue that public institutions must fulfill one of their primary roles in aiding parents in the difficult job of setting boundaries for children. This is partially accomplished by including only orderly, selected knowledge on their library shelves or in curricula. Although it is not explicit in challengers' discourse, the question of selection and whose values should be represented in collections and curricula undergirds many of challengers' arguments. As shown in the analysis, challengers view the librarians and administrators of public institutions as proxies for community opinion, and these selectors' decisions should match those of the community as a whole.

Parenting—A Difficult Boundary-Setting Role

Challengers typify parenting as one of the most important roles in society that requires special skills and resources that some parents are unable to provide to their children. Their discourse concerning the role of parenting is somewhat fraught. Parenting is "natural" in that it should be obvious how one should conduct oneself as a parent, particularly when it comes to setting boundaries for one's children. However, the challengers also argue that parenting is also a skill that can be learned if one is willing to be attentive. In either case, challengers contend that it is imperative for parents to fulfill their role as boundary setters for their children. The job of parenting is also fraught for challengers because they tend to view parents as having exclusive control over their children's lives when it comes to access to difficult knowledge. If one of the primary roles of a parent is to maintain boundaries, it is clearly problematic for challengers that there are parents who do not agree with them on what those boundaries ought to be. These parents are essentially "falling down on the job." When faced with such disagreement, the challengers turn to institutions for help.

When it comes to the role of public institutions vis-à-vis the role of parents, challengers argue that public libraries and schools should help parents provide boundaries for their children. This means that they should always err on the side of caution. The presence of objectionable material on library shelves or school curricula means that they are not fulfilling this role. The construction of these institutions in challengers' discourse will be discussed in more detail in the following chapter.

Childhood—Innocent Vessels of Knowledge

The innocence of children, a structuring structure that centers on a particular construction of childhood that dominates in our society, is a major theme in challengers' discourse. In this formulation, innocence is understood as a lack of knowing about ideas or issues that are perceived to be negative. Unless they are introduced to it by outsiders through media or the educational curriculum, children do not know about sexuality, obscenity, or violence. Most of the challengers do not view these as part of the human condition—they are solely learned behaviors. Children's innocence must be protected by both parents and institutions. The challenged material signifies the presence of knowledge that is forbidden for children and if they are not exposed to the material, their innocence will be maintained. This is what it means to set boundaries for children as a parent. By setting limits parents are, in fact, protecting their children's innocence.

What is most significant here is that children are not understood as individuals who possess the ability to have critical distance from texts. Since, according to challengers, children lack the interpretive strategies to properly understand the challenged material, it will necessarily lead to dire consequences if they are exposed to it. Part of what it means to be a child is to lack adequate skills of comprehension when faced with problematic material. Everything to which children are exposed becomes part of their character. When encountering such a signifier, challengers draw on the discourses of childhood innocence that structure their own worldviews to justify their arguments for relocation or removal of objectionable material. In fact, the loss of innocence in childhood is explicitly linked to the overall moral decline in society. As the concerned grandmother in Lewiston, Maine, notes:

> Lewiston Public Library shows no remorse nor makes inquiries to the cost of sexual liberation of youth as is revealed by experts.
>
> Youth who grasp the essence of their human nature will never be a detriment to society. Youth have the capacity to achieve true meaning of their human sexuality, and of being other-centered for the building up and protection of society. Impede their natural growth and development and we destroy local culture and beyond.
>
> I cannot possibly bring into this report every credible piece of evidence [that] leads to what does not keep our youth safe, but I've made a diligent effort [to] gather the facts needed to get the book "It's Perfectly Normal" off the shelves of public funded libraries and out of schools. (Book challenge letter, Lewiston, ME, January 30, 2008)

This quote clearly demonstrates the consequences of not removing the challenged material from the library shelves. Children who are exposed to the material will not grow up to be productive members of society. As a consequence, not only will the local community be destroyed but also the larger society. The cost of "sexual liberation" for is simply too high. It should be noted that these ideas are not necessarily grounded in empirical ideas but simply reflect how childhood is currently constructed in our society. As previously discussed, Kerry Robinson notes that the ideas that adults attempt to censor tend to be difficult knowledge or "knowledge that many adults find challenging to address in their own lives but especially with children."[8] In some respects, challengers argue that it is public institutions' role to ensure that they will not have to discuss difficult knowledge with their children. This also helps to explain why some books are targeted and not others. The following chapter describes in more detail challengers' descriptions of what happens when a reader encounters such knowledge.

NOTES

1. Jessica G., "Remember That Wisconsin Woman Arrested for Overdue Books?" *Jezebel* (blog), August 28, 2008, accessed July 24, 2014, http://jezebel.com/5043035/.

2. Emily J. M. Knox, "The Challengers of West Bend: The Library as a Community Institution," in *Libraries and the Reading Public in Twentieth-Century America*, ed. Christine Pawley and Louise S. Robbins (Madison: University of Wisconsin Press, 2013), 200–16.

3. Michael Warner, "Publics and Counterpublics," *Public Culture* 14, no. 1 (2002): 49–90.

4. This is in keeping with the U.S. Supreme Court's decision in *Board of Education, Island Trees Union Free School District No. 26 v. Pico* (No. 80-2043), which held that banning books due to objectionable material in public school libraries is a violation of students' First Amendment rights.

5. This action is against the ALA Code of Conduct. The *Intellectual Freedom Manual* states that school libraries should follow all school policies but information regarding students' reading should be protected. American Library Association, *Intellectual Freedom Manual*, 8th ed. (Chicago: American Library Association, 2010).

6. Stephen Colclough, *Consuming Texts: Readers and Reading Communities, 1695–1870* (New York: Palgrave Macmillan, 2007).

7. For a historical analysis of childhood innocence, and its relationship to media consumption, see Nicola Beisel, *Imperiled Innocents: Anthony Comstock and Family Reproduction in Victorian America* (Princeton, NJ: Princeton University Press, 1997).

8. Kerry H. Robinson, *Innocence, Knowledge, and the Construction of Childhood: The Contradictory Nature of Sexuality and Censorship in Children's Contemporary Lives* (London: Routledge, 2013), 8.

Chapter Five

Reading Should Edify the Soul

COPS AT THE BANNED BOOK GIVEAWAY

"Meridian Police Show Up to Free Book Giveaway" was the headline on KBOI Radio's website in Meridian, Idaho.[1] *Raw Story*'s headline stated, "Concerned Idaho Citizen Calls Police over Public Banned Book Giveaway to High School Students" while *Wonkette*'s weekly Derp Roundup blared, "Idaho Parents Call Cops to Protect Children from Banned Book."[2] Once again, soon after law enforcement was involved in some fashion, a book banning made the national news. Although the Meridian case, like the one in Lewiston, Maine, also involves a concerned grandmother, the outcome was decidedly different. In Meridian, the local school district included Sherman Alexie's novel *The Absolutely True Diary of a Part-Time Indian* on its 10th-grade recommended book list. Then during fhe 2013–2014 school year, a concerned grandmother asked the district to remove the book from the list. At the hearing on April 1, 2014, she argued that

> it is not the school's responsibility to teach our children empathy. It is not the teacher's responsibility to feel that they are in control of our children. These children came from our wombs. You have them, as teachers, for a small part of the day. We have them for a lifetime and I do not want our children exposed to explicit, filthy, racist things. Please do the courageous thing and remove this book from the curriculum.[3]

After two hours of public testimony, the board voted 2–1 to retain a hold that they had already placed on the book. According to news reports, Alexie's book was not removed from library shelves but the district was seeking a replacement for the recommended reading list. The book giveaway was held in response to the board's decision after two women in the neighboring state of Washington raised money to purchase 350 copies of the book. They encouraged Meridian students to visit a local park on April 23, World Book Day, to obtain a free copy. A junior at the local high school gave out the books. Then, about an hour into the giveaway, the police stopped by to investigate. They had received calls that a "banned book" was being given out at the park and students were picking up the book without their parents' permission. The police "found nothing wrong with what was going on in the park."[4]

How can we understand this response to giving away Alexie's book? What would lead someone to feel that the appropriate response to a book giveaway would be to call the police? As noted in chapter 1, the discourse of censorship reveals the link between power and knowledge. This chapter focuses on the second part of the equation, knowledge. One of the challengers in Clarkstown, New York, stated that the books should be for "the edification of our children" (Request for reconsideration #1, Clarkstown, NY, date redacted [February 2011]). This need for edifying media is a common theme in contemporary American evangelical Christian culture. To edify is to improve moral character, and the concept of only exposing oneself to media that "edifies" is a common topic of discussion in sermons and blogs.[5] Although all challengers are not evangelical Christians and do not use religious language in their arguments, one theme that is common in much of their discourse is that media should improve character and interpreting texts is directly related to edifying the soul. The story of the Meridian book challenger and the community members who called the police about the book giveaway demonstrates that there are some who fear what the consequences will be if teenagers are exposed to the knowledge contained in *The Absolutely True Diary of a Part-Time Indian*. Where does this fear come from? What might these consequences be? This chapter explores some answers to these questions through the lens of print culture and the practice of reading.

Knowledge, as acquired through the reading of books, is the primary focus of this chapter. In particular, it centers on three aspects of knowledge, its transmission, and interpretation as it pertains to the discourse of censorship. As stated in chapter 2, an interpretive strategy is defined within this study as a set of decisions, based on one's worldview, regarding analysis that one makes both before and during the act of reading. The interpretive strategies that one finds in challengers' discourse focus on a mimetic, literal interpretation of texts. The chapter first explores the idea of the book as a transmitter of knowledge and therefore an object of concern for challengers. In particular the chapter focuses on how challengers construct the book as both a material object and how the knowledge contained within is reified by its presence in a book. Second, the chapter discusses the various interpretive strategies that are common in challengers' discourse. Third, the chapter investigates the perceived effects of reading on the character and behavior of children. Finally, the chapter explores how challengers employ causal arguments to justify the removal or relocation of books in public institutions.

WHY BOOKS MATTER

Is it possible that there is something significant about the book as an object that informs challengers' efforts? Although there are some challenges against video games and DVDs in public institutions, none of these reaches the numbers of challenges to books. The idea of the book plays a significant part in their challengers' worldview. Challengers rarely discuss books as such; however, it is clear that the construction of the book as a material object is of great importance to understanding both their actions and their discourse. As will be demonstrated below, it is not mere happenstance that challengers target books, as books are integral to the writing's work as an indexical sign. In challengers' discourse there is a strong correlation between the writing in books and truth. Although there are other formats and types of media that contain texts, for challengers, the texts contained in the form of books have a special significance. These texts are capable of changing lives and therefore should contain timeless truths.

In order to conceptualize how challengers construct their idea of the book, the interviews with challengers began with questions regarding the importance of books in their lives. The Central York, Pennsylvania, interviewee discusses a book that she read in her childhood that led her to become an environmentalist:

> You know, I started living to read when I was really young and I remember reading a book in 5th grade called *The Field*. It really opened my eyes to a whole world that I didn't know existed about cruelty and things like that. So I became very conscious of being more protective of animals and endangered species and the environment. That's kind of been a lifelong thing that's been part of me. Part of my interest back then and enjoy it today. Sounds very simple and simplistic but it is something I remember very well.
>
> At this time I had never really heard of anything like that, I never knew that kind of thing existed and went on in the world. So I became a member of Greenpeace after that and sort of followed up with PETA after that. In high school I did not pursue the dissection of the pig and that kind of thing. It gave me a little something to look at—there's more to the world than what's going on in our little town. (Interview with challenger, Central York, PA, December 7, 2011)

Although this does not specifically discuss books as books, it does clarify how important reading and, by implication books themselves, can be in someone's life. Discourse concerning the importance of reading is common in contemporary society, and the language used throughout this response is strikingly deliberate. The interviewee states that she started "living to read" as a young person and that her exposure to environmentalism at such a young age became a part of her overall character. In some respects she became a different person because of her exposure to this book. This statement defines a core theme in challengers' discourse—books can change lives in both positive and negative directions, and reading can change one's life. It is not that other media cannot have this same life-changing effect, but that books, in particular, can have a profound and formative effect on readers. This helps to contextualize the actions of challengers with regard to books in public institutions. Books—as books—matter. Another interviewee states, "I'm a Christian so the Bible, of course, changed my life" (Interview with challenger, Helena, MT, December 12, 2011). As discussed in chapter 2, Baruch Spinoza argued that meaning cannot be separated from the materiality of the text. "The disposition of these letters produces effects in my mind and in my body."[6] This study argues that because challengers are confident that books can change lives, it is very important that texts that are contained within shape one's moral character in a positive direction.

One challenger offers a clear account of the place of books within the marketplace of ideas. For her, concepts and ideas, if they are good, will be presented over and over again through various media. That is, the good ideas will become more popular and others will fall away. What matters most to the challenger is how the ideas are presented within this marketplace:

> It's true this particular book has valid points to make, but it's not as if the baby is being thrown out with the bath water. Ideas are not babies; they are fluid. If an idea is good and important, it will surface again in better surroundings. I'm certain other books make similar worthy observations without pushing our children in for yet another dip into the gutter. Time is short. With a wondrous array of great books and great ideas available, why should one moment be wasted on a book that may do more harm than good? (Letter to the board, Helena, MT, December 3, 2010)

Interestingly, this is similar to Mill's argument in *On Liberty*.

For this challenger and others, it is not the ideas in the challenged book that are necessarily harmful, but how they are presented to children. For this challenger, there are other books that discuss the same ideas in a more respectable fashion and good ideas will appear in books that do not have objectionable content. These are "better surroundings" that the challenger discusses above. In the marketplace of ideas, there are many ways to present various concepts and it is best to do this in the most positive manner possible.

It seems that part of the reason why books, in particular, are the target of censors is that once one has access to a book, it cannot be censored unless the book is taken away from the reader. This, of course, goes back to historical models of the practice of reading including silent reading and the lack of an outside interpreter between the reader and the text. Although it is possible to censor books through redaction, this is not discussed by challengers in the research presented here. There have been some cases of textbooks being marked through as a result of challenges but none of the challengers in this study suggested this tactic. It might be that the marking through printed texts has strong negative implications for the challengers and is tied to their reverence for the book as a material object. Since challengers usually do not advocate the redaction of texts, the relationship between the reader and the text is unmediated by other interpreters. As discussed in chapter 2, reading silently is a private act in which the reader interacts with an unmediated text. There is no way of knowing what one is reading (that is, one's position in the text) or imparting suggestions for interpretation of the texts. One challenger notes:

> Of all the tremendous literary works that could be presented for the edification of our children, why would something so destructive to the hearts and minds of young people be selected? The media trough [*sic*] the television "bleeps" foul language. Evidently there is still some moral standard by which modern day society follows. When a book of this sort is presented, there is no way to limit or sensor [*sic*] the content. (Request for reconsideration #1, Clarkstown, NY, date redacted [February 2011])

Books, unlike broadcast media, are not censored for language. Whatever is in the text is seen by the reader regardless of whether or not the reader possesses adequate interpretive strategies to interpret it. As the letter writer states, "there is no way to censor the content" once it is in the reader's hands.

Books are also constructed as powerful vehicles for knowledge and operate as legitimizers of texts. For challengers, these characteristics mean that the ideas contained within books must be morally sound. The responsibility for this rests with both authors and publishers. Challengers find it surprising that authors would take the time to write material that they consider inappropriate and, following this first offense of writing the work, it is even more outrageous that a publisher would legitimize the writing by publishing the manuscript. Both authors and publishing companies are blamed for allowing such ideas to reach such a revered medium. The following challenger questions the motivations of the author on one of the themes of the book regarding the misuse of power by one of the characters:

> On the form it is asked what we believed the theme of this book is. We heard of the misuse of power along with others, however, those supporting this book don't seem to want to ask how a 12-year-old lusting after his aunt, getting sexually stirred at the thought of a young girl being sexually abused by her uncle, among others, fit into this novel. These things are very disturbing and I would question the author's mindset and what he was thinking by putting these

things in the book, as they have nothing to do with the misuse of power.
(Letter to the board, Merrill, WI, June 15, 2011)

This challenger argues that authors, through the act of writing and publishing, have power and by writing an inappropriate book, the author has
abused his privilege to influence the minds of young people. This perception
that authors have great influence over the minds of their readers is based in a
particular understanding of the practice of reading. The following section
explores how challengers construct the process of reading—that is, the interpretive strategies that one uses to make meaning out of text.

INTERPRETING TEXT

Understanding the process of interpreting text is crucial to understanding the
actions of challengers. Challengers tend to describe interpretation in "commonsense" terms that discount the possibility that a single text might give
rise to many different interpretations. As noted in chapter 2, this elevation of
monosemic interpretive strategies is strongly influenced by the Common
Sense philosophical tradition that emphasizes the importance of experience
and the accessibility of truth that might be found in a particular text. Although challengers do not, of course, directly state that their construction of
reading is grounded in this philosophical tradition, it is clear from their
discourse that texts "mean what they say and say what they mean." That is,
there is little possibility for interpreting texts using metaphorical or symbolic
strategies. This particular interpretive strategy is also linked to a particular
understanding of the effects of reading. Since, as challengers argue, commonsense interpretive strategies that emphasize literalism dominate, the effects of the text on the reader are intensified. This starts with a particular
understanding of how the imagination works.

Mind Movies and Mimesis

For challengers, one issue of great importance concerns the workings of the
imagination and the imagination's relationship to interactions of the mind
with text. Challengers' discourse includes many references to the act of
constructing mental images of what happens in the text while one is reading.
One challenger uses a list of class discussion questions as comparison to his
understanding of the practice of reading:

"1. Remind your child that when making a picture or mental image, readers
put themselves in the story or text by making a mind movie." When you really
enjoy what you are reading creating this picture is probably the most important
step. But do we really want our kids, even if they are age 15 or 16, picturing
themselves in *Montana 1948*? Or do we want them making it into a mind

movie? We sure don't. We hope you will agree and remove this book. (Letter
to the board, Merrill, WI, September 27, 2011)

The process of reading as a mimetic activity is very clearly articulated by
this challenger. When someone reads, he or she creates images or "mind
movies" and, for this challenger, the pictures created by the challenged book
are unacceptable. This evocative term gives some insight into how challengers understand how the imagination works. Note that this is not just true of
children but of readers in general. It also harkens back to the protection of
children theme discussed in chapter 4, that there are some ideas and concepts
available in the marketplace of ideas that children simply do not need to
know. This is a clear definition of difficult or forbidden knowledge. As
another challenger states, such images and knowledge can "warp" children
for the rest of their lives:

> Finally, the tragedy is that scores of minors are having their minds warped and
> corrupted by images and themes they'll remember for the rest of their lives.
> Images and themes that scintillate and seduce. Images and themes they are
> entirely unqualified and unprepared to handle or process. (Request for recon-
> sideration #1, Clarkstown, NY, date redacted [February 2011])

Note that for this challenger, children lack critical distance from the text,
defined here as proper interpretive skills for understanding the objectionable
material, and are simply unable to cope with the images presented in the
challenged book. If they do encounter them, they will be scarred forever.
Challengers' conceptualizations of the lingering effects of such images will
be discussed in more detail below.

Children are corrupted through texts because images remain in their
minds and cannot be erased. This links back to the definitions of innocence
described in chapter 4. Note that challengers employ both the tabula rasa and
latent definitions throughout their discourse. One challenger compares texts
to Pandora's box:

> Anyone going in there can just take that book out. And then they're going
> to . . . those doors are open. It's like a Pandora's box or whatever. You can't go
> back once you've had that information in your head. That's it. That will lead to
> further curiosity about things. And I don't know what that means. Does that
> mean acting it out? Doing it with another . . . to see . . . or whatever. I have no
> idea, but I don't think those things are appropriate for children that young.
> (Interview with challenger, Carrollton, TX, January 3, 2012)

Not only do texts expose children to images that will become a permanent
part of their being, this challenger argues that the images also lead them
down a path toward an unspecified danger. This is the negative, mimetic
interpretation of text that leads to sin as described in chapter 2 wherein the

effect of reading a particular text is a pathway to moral corruption. Although the challenger quoted above cannot quite verbalize what might happen if a child were to read the challenged text, there is an overwhelming sense that the effects will be negative and lead to the dissolution of the natural order.

Another challenger describes the process of reading more obliquely; however, he also demonstrates a particular understanding of the imagination:

> Because teenage suicide is an issue. Those kids need an answer. The theme promoted in this book, of course we can't talk about it. We can give it to our kids. They can envision it. They can live through it. But we can't talk about it because we're adults. Unbelievable. (Male speaker #1, Book challenge hearing, Merrill, WI, September 29, 2011)

This is striking testimony regarding the power of the imagination. The challenger states that there is a direct correlation between imagining and experience. Envisioning an event through text is understood to not simply be an experience of the mind but an event that one "lives through." Reading is constructed as a mimetic process wherein the act of imagining the events of the text is the same as living it. For this challenger, when children read about teenage suicide it is not merely a description of an action by a character in a novel—they empathetically experience suicide themselves. These ideas are based in a particular interpretive strategy rooted in "commonsense" interpretation of the text in which words "mean what they say."

Commonsense and Truth

As noted, texts "saying what they mean" or a "commonsense" interpretation of texts is found throughout challengers' discourse. Challengers do not allow for varying interpretations of text especially where children are concerned. Children, and sometimes youth, who are considered to have undisciplined imaginations and lack critical distance from texts, are subject to give highly literal interpretations of text. Texts are a medium wherein "what you see is what you get"—the words on the page both mean what they say and say what they mean. Texts are a monosemic media (i.e., they possess a stable referent) and can only be interpreted in one way. As George Marsden notes, "Mystical, metaphorical and symbolic perceptions of reality have largely disappeared."[7] This construction of texts as literal and monosemic is found throughout challengers' discourse.

The interviewee in Helena, Montana, described commonsense interpretation more colloquially as "garbage in, garbage out." Although the following quote is lengthy, it elucidates a particular understanding of how texts can be interpreted.

Right. The school should not require it. Kids can read . . . in my family we strongly discourage reading stuff like that. We truly believe "garbage in, garbage out." Other kids. Other homes. Other families. You know, want to say what they can do or whatever . . .

Well . . . my family has a different definition of what garbage is. And that became clear going through this process. I felt like a freak. And what I think is garbage is not considered garbage to most people out there. We are just very concerned about what we let our kids watch. What we let them read. What we let them see and hear. We believe that the cussing, the sexual innuendo, the gutter language, and the visual on TV. You know all that you see on TV. The sexual the inappropriate, the potty humor, we consider that garbage. And when we take that in, through our eyes, through our hearts, our ears. And then that's what comes out. In the way we behave and the way we speak and the way we treat other people. That's what we mean by garbage in garbage out. (Interview with challenger, Helena, MT, December 12, 2011)

For the challenger, certain texts are "garbage" because they contain, for example, objectionable language or sexual situations.[8] This can also be linked to the idea of the necessity for texts to edify, as described above. If children are exposed to these texts, they will then have a penchant for such obscenity and sexuality. The challenger makes little room for texts that might use vulgarity or obscenity as part of a cautionary tale or as a marker of realism. Books and other media that do not build strong moral character in a very literal and mimetic sense are to be avoided at all costs.

In the following lengthy exchange, the challenger attempts to read some of the more salacious parts of Alexie's book at a challenge hearing in West-field, New Jersey. It is presented as a dialogue for clarity.

Challenger: That's why the book has to be made optional for parents who are unhappy with their children being exposed to it. I don't think people really . . . people are really in favor of the book and I don't think they know some of the sections and they're pretty brutal. And let me read an excerpt. One of the students read an excerpt. This is a good one. [Quoting] "I love that tree," I said. "That's because you're a tree fag," Rowdy said. "I'm not a tree fag," I said. "Then how come you like to stick your dick in knotholes?" [p. 225]

Other attendee: We've already done this!

Challenger: You heard this already. So am I being censored then.

Other attendee: No.

Challenger: Is this something you don't want to hear. Is that offensive to anyone.

Other attendee: Not offended.

Challenger: Not offended. Everybody's happy with this? What to go some more? Want to go to the masturbation section.

Other attendee: What's your point?

Challenger: That there are very offensive—

Other attendee: Read out of context.

Board president: Excuse me, one second.

Challenger: There are very offensive sections of this book.

[Unintelligible from crowd] [Gavel bang]

Board president: Excuse me. You're welcome to speak. It's your turn to speak. People in the audience please keep your comments until it's your turn to speak. [Name] we're good.

Challenger: My point is that there are segments of this book that are difficult to argue that some parents could be offended by it and don't want their children exposed to it. That position has to be respected. There's no doubt about it. I could go on. I have a whole bunch of paper clips here. Nobody wants to hear it. Sooo. They're so offensive nobody wants to hear it. But parents have a right to not want to subject their children to those sentiments in the ninth grade. (Male speaker #1, Book challenge hearing, Westfield, NJ, February 28, 2012)

Although the challenger is clearly attempting to get a rise out of his fellow hearing attendees, it is also clear that for him, these sections of the book are on their face offensive. He is incredulous that others at the hearing would not agree with him. For him, there is no possibility that the sections he is reading might be a marker of realism or might employ an interpretive lens other than titillation.

Another issue for challengers is the inappropriateness of dark literature. Often associated with realistic fiction, the prevalence of dark themes in books for teens was the subject of a much discussed editorial by Katie Roiphe in the *Wall Street Journal*.[9] One challenger agrees with Roiphe's assessment that such literature is too bleak:

The young adult branch of literature, like anything else, has its good and its bad sides. We do not need to cater to a teens need to be entertained by viewing or reading salacious, or gritty, material to gain their attention. I understand the idea of reaching out to them where they are and to real situations that go on in their lives, but not at the expense of letting our schools, or them, wallow in it. They need a contrast to that situation. Something that challenges their thinking and to influence them to deal with life situations in a more positive way. (Letter to the board, Merrill, WI, June 10, 2011)

For this challenger, reading material should be challenging but positive. Since teens are, by nature, "salacious" (a conceptualization of childhood discussed in chapter 4), adults must be sure that the texts that teens read are realistic but not to the point that they do not provide some sort of positive instruction for life.

In some respects, commonsense interpretation is directly linked to education and instruction. Texts, for challengers, are a priori instructional—they should teach people the right way to live. This educational aspect seems to be linked to books as a material object and is, in fact, the primary purpose for literature:

> I have spent my whole life working with children. And I can tell you that the things that what we expose our children to does not make it right and does not necessarily prepare them for life and to make good decisions. If I want my kid to know more about drugs do I then get heroin or cocaine and say "Try it son"? Or try it on my daughters? But when it comes to literature, [it's] okay? We have this thing where we want to educate. (Male speaker #3, Book challenge hearing, Clarkstown, NY, March 24, 2011)

For this challenger, books that discuss heroin and cocaine are implicitly teaching the reader how to take drugs. This is similar to the issue of imagination discussed above; literature must not contain certain themes or images because reading about an experience is the same as having it. Here we see a clear demonstration of the perceived lack of critical distance between the reader and the text, and reading becomes an imitative endeavor.

The theme of commonsense reading strategies is most fully elucidated when challengers discuss objectionable sections of the challenged book. Texts are understood literally and, as a consequence, there is no concept of multiple layers of meaning or polysemy. The following passage from a challenger's letter discusses some of the events in Sherman Alexie's coming-of-age novel, *The Absolutely True Diary of a Part-Time Indian*. The writer is discussing the 14-year-old protagonist of the novel and quotes from the book:

> (He is proud to masturbate; he is good at it and he is ambidextrous) and "if God didn't want us to masturbate he wouldn't have given us thumbs"—and later "you should read and draw because really good books and cartoons give you a boner." Then still later he talks of getting an erection because the teacher was so good looking. He later tells his friend he is a "fag tree." I thought we

were trying to teach our children not to use those "bullying terms"? (Letter to
the board, Helena, MT, n.d.)

Since the book uses the term "fag," then the school is teaching students
that it is permissible to use the term "fag." Note that the challenger does not
state that the book might discuss how it feels to be called such a derogatory
name or that the book may be using the term to create a realistic atmosphere—the focus is on the use of the term itself. This concept of learning
proper morals through text is found throughout challengers' arguments. For
example, challengers' discourse links commonsense interpretation to the educational purpose of literature. For them, reading about something means
that it is being "promoted":

> It seems strange and fickle to on the one hand, observe the school district adopt
> safe-sex teaching practices for high school age children, and yet have no
> qualms about presenting material such as this book. When STDs, unwanted
> pregnancies, and even suicide is on the rise, how could the promotion of the
> Images [*sic*] portrayed on the pages of this book, be good for our children? Just
> because "it's out there"—the internet etc.— does that mean it should be pro-
> moted by those who are entrusted to be wise guides in the maturation process
> of our children? (Request for reconsideration #1, Clarkstown, NY, date re-
> dacted [February 2011])

For the challenger, all educational materials across the school curriculum are
interpreted by children and youth the same way. The materials used in the
English classroom and the sex education classroom will be interpreted by
students using the same strategies. Note the conflation of text and images in
the challenger's statement. Reading about an action in prose is the same as
having it presented as "mind movies."

Here we see a conflation of nonfiction (which one presumes would be
used in a sex education class) and fiction. This lack of separation between
fiction and nonfiction is common throughout challengers' discourse and relates to the idea of commonsense interpretive strategies. As noted in chapter
2, there is a strong correlation in challengers' discourse between the written
word and truth. For example, in the following quote, the challenger argues
that the author Alexie must write the truth in his novel:

> Wow, OK. Number 1: Highly inappropriate material for a high school English
> Literature class. especially the immature and crass way with which he speaks.
> Number 2: Again. Disrespect of women. Alexie endorses objectifying women.
> Using them to satisfy his own sexual desires. Number 3: Blanket false state-
> ments. "Everybody does it"? That's a lie. I know of many parents that are
> teaching their children differently. They are teaching them a more excellent
> way. Not everybody does it. But can you imagine young, impressionable teen-
> agers believing these inaccurate observations? Also, "If God hadn't wanted us

to masturbate. then God wouldn't have given us thumbs." Another big fat lie. (Letter to the board, Helena, MT, n.d.)

The use of the term "lie" in this statement is instructive. For this challenger, it seems that fictional texts must be factually "true." It is important to remember that the quotes given in the statement above are from a work of fiction and, presumably, the author is not arguing that the narrator's voice is "true," but this is how they are interpreted by the challenger. This is an example of commonsense interpretation where the author "means" what he writes.

For other challengers, there is less of a conflation between fiction and nonfiction and more of a focus on the concept of "timeless truths." The capitalization in the following quotation is the writer's own:

> That the author writes well and makes some valid points is sadly offset by various inappropriate discussions including the teen's ideas about masturbation which are as follows: "EVERYBODY does it. And EVERYBODY likes it. And if God hadn't wanted us to masturbate, then God wouldn't have given us thumbs. So thank God for my thumbs." [10] As I said, this book discusses things that are morally erosive. Why should any child or teenager be required to wallow in the immoral reality of this fictional boy's life? (Letter to the board, Helena, MT, n.d.)

The juxtaposition of "immoral reality" and "fictional boy" is striking in this statement. One might surmise that, for this challenger, fiction must present a moral reality and an appropriate blueprint for action. This particular book, according to the challenger, does neither.

This line of reasoning regarding truth is also discussed by other challengers. The nature of truth in texts means that books must contain a moral lesson. The following challenger begins by discussing the negative influences of inappropriate texts:

> When children "must read" fiction or other books containing degrading material at school, they can assume that such content is approved by both the school and society. This also has the possibility of setting the stage for influencing our children in a negative way by giving them permission to not only read, but, to act out immoral (non-acceptable) situations. "Bad behavior" (non-acceptable) does have consequences and influences others. This is overlooked in *Montana 1948* when evil deeds, including murder, rape, etc., escape punishment. (Letter to the board, Merrill, WI, June 13, 2011)

Once again, there is a prevailing theme that including a particular book in the curriculum means that everything in the book is endorsed by the community. For this challenger, one of the primary problems with the challenged book is that it does not present adequate consequences for objectionable behavior.

The book must present truths, and one aspect of "truth" for this challenger is that there should be clear and direct consequences for poor behavior. Without this, the book is not "true" and should not be included in the curriculum as it is poor instructional material.

Since children lack critical distance from the text and interpretive skill, they will interpret the text as meaning that such behavior is permitted. They lack the interpretive strategies to understand what they are reading because they are still maturing and therefore must read books that will give them a good moral foundation. One challenger refers to scientific studies on child development to describe the concept of critical distance:

> Most students would gravitate toward this book. Is it our role to use this book? We understand what is happening in their lives. Some of the children who are still forming have not fully formed their position. They are looking to adults for good examples. We don't want them calling out and using this language. We have to protect students. (Request for reconsideration #1, Clarkstown, NY, date redacted [February 2011])

Here the concept of having a "fully formed position" might be understood as a type of critical distance, and children do not possess the interpretive strategies to understand what they are reading. They are still maturing and therefore must read books that will give them a good moral foundation. Another challenger refers to scientific studies on child development to describe the concept of critical distance:

> Studies on brain research show that the human brain, particularly the frontal lobe (where judgment is made), is not fully developed until 22 to 25 years of age. Why are we subjecting our children to immoral situations and illegal acts when they are not ready to process it? (Request for reconsideration #1, Clarkstown, NY, date redacted [February 2011])

Children are simply unable to process the material found in the challenged book. For this challenger, until they are ready to do so they should not be subjected to the themes in the text.

Also of interest is the idea that reading the texts can lead to a particular behavior. Another challenger states this idea plainly:

> Has anyone ever challenged you to be a defender of women and children? I hope this is not a pleading that you've heard for the first time. The truth is the contents of the book in question leads to a lot of misery, pain, lack of freedom, and often death. Consequences of the behaviors taught in the book, and there are many, obviously not even taken into consideration. How responsible is that!!? (Letter to the board, Lewiston, ME, August 20, 2007)

The concept of direct and knowable reading effects is found throughout challengers' discourse and is strongly linked to commonsense interpretation and children's lack of critical distance. Since texts "say what they mean" and children do not have the skills to interpret them using a different method, reading inappropriate texts will inevitably lead to inappropriate, imitative behavior.

THE CONSEQUENCES OF READING

Challengers construct reading as a practice that has effects on individuals' behavior and moral character.[11] Texts are not read passively but, as mentioned above, they can alter a person's life and can have both long- and short-term effects. This section of the chapter focuses on the discourse employed to describe both of these sets of consequences. Generally, when challengers describe the long-term effects of reading, the language is stark and more concerned with permanent psychological and spiritual damage. Short-term effects, on the other hand, are discussed using what one might call "triggering" language. Once again, there is little nuance in the discourse concerning reading effects—reading inappropriate material will inexorably lead to both inappropriate behavior and poor moral character.

One of the interesting aspects of the Merrill, Wisconsin, request for reconsideration form is that it specifically asks the requestor to describe what effects the book will have on someone who reads it. Challengers provided a variety of responses to the question "What do you feel might be the result of reading, viewing or listening to this material?" None of these challengers wrote that there would not be negative effects if children were exposed to the book in question. Below are a few of the replies that some of the challengers gave:

> It stimulates the imagination toward sexual behavior as well as violence being a suggested way to release this feeling—Rape. (Request for reconsideration, Merrill, WI, June 7, 2011)
> While a 12 year old boy realistically may not be able to articulate his feelings some young person reading this could be sexually aroused. It adds to all the X-rated things thrown at young people—Not Good. (Request for reconsideration, Merrill, WI, May 31, 2011)
> It gives their minds immorality to think of. It paints filth in their imagination. It pulls their morals down. (Request for reconsideration, Merrill, WI, June 15, 2011)
> It lends itself to putting unnecessary sexual thoughts in young people's minds. It also lends itself to let kids know if they make mistakes/kill yourself. (Request for reconsideration, Merrill, WI, June 13, 2011)

The explicit details in this book create visual images that a child under 18 does not need to be and should not be exposed to. (Request for reconsideration, Merrill, WI, June 11, 2011)

Although many different themes (some of which have been previously discussed) are articulated by the statements above, they are all focused on the effects of reading objectionable materials: The imagination will be used for sexual exploration and possible violence. Children will develop poor moral character and they will not be exposed to proper consequences for objectionable behavior. Children simply do not possess the critical distance or interpretive skill to process what they will read in the book. Of particular interest is that these effects are taken for granted throughout challengers' discourse. Exposure to the challenged book will inevitably lead to the negative effects in the long term, such as the destruction of the soul and, in the short term, embarrassment and acting out.

Corrosion of the Soul

When challengers discuss the long-term effects of reading objectionable material, they often state that they are not only trying to save children's minds but also their souls:

I believe that this book does damage to people especially young, developing maturing children in what that cannot be measured. Reading filth corrodes our souls. I felt dirty reading this book. I'm fully aware that such language is spoken in our kids' culture, But must we, as educators, role models, and monitors, perpetuate it in our schools. (Request for reconsideration, Helena, MT, October 28, 2010)

This is connected to the "garbage in, garbage out" edification argument discussed above. Even though obscenity is common in contemporary culture, reading a text with such language damages the soul. The martial language used here, to be discussed in more detail in the following chapter, is a common characteristic when challengers discuss the long-term effects of reading:

The battle we are engaged in is a battle of our age, to save the minds and souls of the generation. We all need to be very careful of the words and thoughts that are being conveyed to young minds. . . . Teachers must be very careful to use resources that they use in the classroom to reinforce the attitudes and behaviors that you want to see prevail in the rest of areas of the school environment. Using books that might be [?] and unacceptable under school policies sends a convoluted message to the students' minds. There is no middle ground before God. Either you are for me or you are against me. For if you are not putting good thoughts into these students minds, you are acting with Satan. (Male speaker #4, Book challenge hearing, Stockton, MO, September 8, 2010)

For this challenger, the act of removing an objectionable book is part of a "war" for children's souls. It is clear that reading the material will do permanent and lasting harm to their characters and therefore the book must be removed. The language of spiritual warfare will be discussed in more detail in the following chapter.

The challenger in Central York, Pennsylvania, also argues that reading the challenged book could cause permanent psychological damage. In the interview, she was particularly concerned with the effects of reading dark literature:

> I think it's damaging for children to read literature, damages them psychologically . . . that literature, not dark as in Harry Potter dark. But dark as in holding a gun to the head and describing holding a knife to a two-year-old's throat. That's just too graphic too much. Crossing a line. If they weren't doing a story about a kidnapping they wouldn't have . . . you know they get kidnapped and trapped in a closet. But it [should] never [cross] that line where somebody is holding a knife to her throat. To me the line has been crossed and I felt like I had to stand up and say my piece about it. (Interview with challenger, Central York, PA, December 7, 2011)

Although she does not specify what kind of psychological damage dark literature will do to a child, she is clearly worried about the long-term effects of reading such literature. There is a point where the text becomes too intense for a child to read and they will either act out the actions that they read about in a text or be psychologically adversely affected by them.

Acting Out, Triggering, and Microaggressions

The impact of reading on children's souls is not the only reading effect that concerns challengers. There is also a pervasive fear that children will act out the scenes that they read in a book:

> We hope you will agree and remove this book. I also strongly urge you to take a close look at what are [*sic*] children are being fed at school and make sure it is something that we want them to recreate in their minds or potentially act out. (Letter to the board, Merrill, WI, September 27, 2011)

It is not only fear of the imagination as described above that concerns challengers but also fear of what children will do when they are aware of particular behaviors. The ideas given to them through books must be sound so that children will not act upon what they read. [12]

One short-term effect that is discussed throughout challengers' discourse is the possibility that reading the challenged material will cause sexual excitement:

I just looked up the Merriam Webster definition—the depiction of erotic behavior (as in pictures or writing) intended to cause sexual excitement. I wanted
to confirm for myself that depicting in writing would fit the definition, but it
also says it must be intended to cause sexual excitement. I would like to
believe that this is not true, but the more that comes out about what our
children are being exposed to in school, I really don't feel I can assume
anything anymore. Whether or not this fits the legal description of pornography, it is not appropriate for children. Why would we want to expose our
children to this? (Letter to the board, Merrill, WI, June 10, 2011)

This challenger is concerned that children will use the challenged book as
erotica. There is an abrupt shift in the statement from defining erotica to
labeling the book in question as pornography. The issue of literature as
pornography will be discussed in more detail in the following section of this
chapter.

The feeling of embarrassment or needing to hide is used by some challengers as proxy for inappropriate material. If one is embarrassed while
reading a particular text, then it contains objectionable material and should
be removed or relocated:

I noticed the older girl in the backseat of the car. And like she knew she was
looking at something that she wasn't supposed to. She was hunched over a bit
and I thought she's probably making something out of nothing because it's a
public library book from the children's section. [I thought,] "There can't be
anything she shouldn't see." And then I asked her if I could look at the book.
She didn't want to at first and then she did. And I could not believe the things
[she was] reading and seeing.

Graphic. Just too much information. Just way too much information. You
know. And anyone I showed the book to then . . . I couldn't give it back to her.
And I had to let her parents know what she had just seen. And um, she thought
it was disgusting and I asked her [a] question about where it was located. And
right there by the little children's books. She was curious about babies I guess,
but this book just went way beyond, the necessary. You know . . . you can be
truthful without being graphic at that age. (Interview with challenger, Carrollton, TX, January 3, 2012)

The challenger knew that something was wrong with the book because
the child in her care was hiding her reading. The child's actions *meant* that
the book was inappropriate. It is implicit in this statement that appropriate
reading materials do not have to be hidden—they can and should be read out
in the open. As noted in chapter 2, silent reading, as opposed to public
reading, has often been associated with suspicion as well as private and
unmediated interpretation. The challenger above gives some indication as to
why this might be so. If the child had been reading the book aloud, presumably she would have stopped when she reached the objectionable material.

The child's embarrassment and the interviewee's subsequent dismay could only take place if the child was reading to herself.

Another short-term effect that challengers discuss is the concept of "stirring" or triggering. That is, the challenged books are so explicit that they will cause children who have experienced, for example, violence at some point in their lives to relive the events:

> The hardest task as a CPW [child protective worker] was working with children who had been sexually abused and after that experience, I wonder how anyone can defend a book that places sexual abuse in the context of ambiguity. Sexual abuse is an unspeakable violation and must always be portrayed as such. On page 121 of *Montana 1948*, the main character David becomes sexually stirred at the thought of a high school girl being sexually abused by his uncle.
>
> This scene alone created a myriad of questions for me: How would reading about how David was aroused by a possible sexual assault teach boys to respect girls? Would girls gain self-esteem by reading about how young women are abused and the malefactor is never brought to justice? How do I hope children cope with their memories of abuse, when they are reminded of them in their English class? How can I approve of this book and then look at my family member knowing that she had been sexually touched by her teacher, sending her on a depressive spiral or my friend who was molested by his pastor, or another family member, by her grandfather, or another friend molested by a trusted adult. What if my child or your child was sexually abused? What would we think of this book in our classroom? (Female speaker #7, Book challenge hearing, Merrill, WI, September 29, 2011)

Although this testimony includes other common themes in challengers' discourse, including the lack of moral clarity appearing in this statement, what is most prominent is the fear that children who have suffered through abuse might not be able to process the events described in the text. The book will instead elicit terrible memories for them. And, to return to the previous theme discussed in this chapter, this triggering effect will be compounded by the fact that the character who abuses the girls in the book is not, according to the challenger, adequately punished.

Some of the reading effects that challengers discuss are of a more generalized nature but still relate to fear that the challenged book will produce negative feelings within the readers. The following challenger describes her daughter's reported emotional state when she read the objectionable material:

> My daughter was courageous enough to discuss how having to read this material makes her feel. [Redacted] reported feeling inferior, embarrassment [*sic*] and misunderstood, she also felt invalidated and stereotyped. In addition there was no effort in her classroom to dispel these stereotypes and negative view of AI/AN [American Indian/Alaska Native] people. One lecture even promoted

an inaccurate view of why "we have reservations." (Letter to the board, Seattle, WA, March 14, 2010)

As with the challenger from Merrill, Wisconsin, directly above, there is concern that reading the text has immediate negative effects on the reader. This challenger in Seattle, Washington, argues that, because of her heritage, her daughter does not have the same experience as others in her class when reading the book. The classroom becomes a space of hostility because the text makes the daughter feel inferior and embarrassed. This challenger argues that reading is not a neutral activity but one that can alter one's state of mind.

In another case, the challenger in the Seattle case uses the term "microaggression," from social psychology, which refers to everyday behaviors that affect the well-being of minorities, to describe the effects of reading the challenged book:

> I did have a courageous conversation with Ms. [Redacted] on Friday afternoon and I appreciate her apology and her genuine interest in addressing this issue. As you know Seattle Public Schools has a tremendous achievement gap with AI/AN youth. This gap continues to widen for a number of reasons and I feel as though this issue I am raising today is a contributing factor. Accumulated micro-aggressions has a detrimental impact on the emotional well being of AI/AN which undeniable affects academic achievement for many of our Native youth. (Letter to the board, Seattle, WA, March 14, 2010)

Although the term "microaggression" has somewhat different connotation from triggering in that it refers to an outside action rather than what happens to the reader himself or herself, it also describes an effect on the reader. For this letter writer, the challenged book negatively contributes to the overall psychological health of the American Indian and Alaska Native community. Microaggressions including, presumably, the availability of the book in question, lead to an inevitable lack of academic achievement within the AI/AN community.

PORNOGRAPHY AND THE "SLIPPERY SLOPE"

The concept of inevitability is also related to what one might call pornography arguments. There is a well-known discourse within contemporary American society that consuming pornography is a kind of domino effect or "slippery slope" toward violence against women.[13] While they are less focused on pornography's presumed harm against women, challengers draw on this argument and state that consumption of inappropriate material is the beginning of a "slippery slope" toward the destruction of one's moral character. This causal argument was most prevalent in the Merrill, Wisconsin, challenge case.[14] It should be noted here that throughout these quotations from challengers, it is the challenged material that is considered to be porno-graphic:

> According to the CDC information, a [causal] link between pornography and sexual offences has been proven through numerous studies and testimonies. Pornography has proven to have a harmful and corrupting influence . . . and I want to have you hear this: there is no guarantee that pornography will not be imitated by sexual offenders. I want to say that in Wisconsin legislative documents . . . crimes against children are in—and children is defined as anyone under 18 years of age—Chapter 948.11. That it speaks to exposing a child to harmful material or harmful descriptions and variations . . . it's the law against pornography.
>
> I want to ask you, are you sure that you want to take the risk in our school district and our classroom and keeping the book in our curriculum based on what I just read? Will you put a student or a child at risk of being raped? Based on this, who's going to monitor the classroom for the students who have been molested, use pornography, or would be influenced by the literary images of this book of a sexually explicit nature. How do you know that it will not be imitated by somebody that you may never know . . . is in the teacher's classroom and would act out on what they read in this book? How are teachers going to find out ahead of time who those students are? (Female speaker #3, Book challenge hearing, Merrill, WI, September 29, 2011)

This speaker begins with information on pornography from a well-respected institution, the Centers for Disease Control, in order to strengthen her argument against the book. By leaving the book in the school, administrators are risking that students will be sent down a path to sexual violence. Because the book is considered to be pornography, it is, in fact, illegal for the school system to retain it. Note that the challenger also describes the triggering effects of the reading material discussed above.

A challenger in Stockton, Missouri, also characterizes objectionable material as pornography. He links this to acts of imaginative visualization described above:

> I recently attended a Protestant youth retreat. We talked about the problems with internet crime. The number one factor that increases the vulnerability of our children to sexual predators was their exposure to vulgar and profane language. We talk about protection tonight. That our teachers are there to protect us. Thank you for protecting our children. When they visualize these acts is that not pornography? Is it not just as pornographic as if they had seen it in person? Or in action in a photograph? I appreciate your leadership. Leadership is action. Leadership is not imposition. The time is always right to do what you did. (Male speaker #9, Book challenge hearing, Stockton, MO, September 8, 2010)

For the challenger, the work in question is pornographic because it leads the reader to visualize sexual acts. The speaker also states that because children are exposed to obscenity they will be more vulnerable to sexual offenders. This is an interesting change to the common structure of the "slippery slope" argument, which usually relates the change in behavior to the consumer alone. Here, consumption also makes the reader more vulnerable to the misdeeds of others.

The challenger in Merrill, Wisconsin, quoted above offers a precise definition of pornography in order to differentiate it from literature:

> When is it okay to give a child or youth pornography? And what is the right thing to do when you find pornography in the hands of a child. The definition of literature is "works having excellent form or expression or dealing with ideas of permanent and lasting interest." Pornography is "the depiction as in writing of erotic behavior defined to cause sexual excitement." Profane is "the impure, treat with irreverence, or debase with unworthy use." Quarantine is "restraint on movements, on persons, or of goods that are intended to prevent the spread of pests or disease." Disease is "an alteration of a living body such as a human body that impairs the function." (Female speaker #3, Book challenge hearing, Merrill, WI, September 29, 2011)

Here, the challenger draws on discourses concerning health to make her argument. Not only is the challenged book characterized as pornography, it is a disease that must not be accessible to children. For this challenger, the text is like a disease that must be literally quarantined.

Another challenger in Merrill, Wisconsin, also offers definitions of literature and pornography to bolster his or her arguments on the request for reconsideration form:[15]

> Literature: all writings considered as having permanent value
> Pornography: writings pictures etc., intended primarily to arouse sexual desire.
> I find nothing of permanent value in *Montana 1948* . . . [illegible] sexually explicit writing. (Request for reconsideration, Merrill, WI , June 7, 2011)

Once again, the book is labeled as pornography and, because it cannot be classified as literature, it should be removed from the school. As noted in chapter 2, challenge cases are focused on how to properly classify texts, and here we see a clear delineation between "literature" and "pornography." For this challenger, there is no ambiguity regarding how the challenged book should be classified.

The following speaker at the Merrill, Wisconsin, hearing is quoted at length as her testimony demonstrates many different aspects of how the arguments concerning the causal effects of pornography are used in challengers' discourse:

As a grandmother I am very concerned about what's going on and as a person who works with decency groups in the surrounding area and throughout the city it's my observation throughout the years that pornography fuels the thirst of addiction in people who are exposed often to sexually explicit materials. Statistics show that pornography is the seventh largest industry in the U.S. [and] that 11-year olds are the average age of exposure to the internet. That 12-year-olds [to] 17 year olds are the largest consumers, and only 25% of youth who receive solicitations on the internet have told their parents. So why do we want to add fuel to the fire.

Many of these people—children—are exposed in their grammar school years and we find that soft pornography which surrounds us in our society as well as hard pornography stimulates early sexual arousal before many are prepared mentally and emotionally to deal with it. And we find that soft pornography does exactly what cigarettes do to marijuana. It often leads to harder materials.

Reading *Montana 1948* is one example of how young people can be easily aroused as can anyone. Statistics will see that they are already exposed so this is just another piece of coal on the fire. To suggest that pornography with[out] pictures could not have an effect on you, including a harmful [effect], is to deny the whole notion of education and to suggest that people are not affected by what they read and see. In that case, Karl Marx's book, *Das Kapital*, the Bible, and the Qur'an or any advertising have no effect either. My suggestion is to remove *Montana 1948* from the curriculum not because it's the wrong thing to do but because it's the right thing to do. (Female speaker #2, Book challenge hearing, Merrill, WI, September 29, 2011)

The speaker begins with statistics that show that children are exposed to pornography on a regular basis and leaving the book in the school system will only increase their consumption. Consuming pornography leads directly to "indecency." Although the speaker allows that there is a difference between what she characterizes as hard and soft pornography (one contains pictures and the other does not), there is no difference in the effects of these two types. She makes an explicit analogy linking pornography and cigarettes as "gateway drugs." Finally, she notes that one should "deny the whole notion of education" if one does not believe that reading has effects. For her, it makes no sense to have students read anything if educators do not think it will affect them in some way. These are, in some sense, "scientific" arguments that the challengers draw on to prove their case for removing, restricting, and relocating objectionable materials.

KNOWLEDGE, COMMONSENSE, AND THE
EFFECTS OF READING

What happens when someone reads? For challengers, the answer to this question is of primary importance. If reading a particular text will lead you astray, then it is best not only to eschew reading it but also to remove or relocate the text so that those who do not have the mental facility to process the information contained within will not have access to it. As demonstrated in this chapter, challengers employ a myriad of arguments related to reading throughout their discourse. First, they view the material object of the book as a powerful medium in and of itself. Second, challengers discuss a variety of interpretive strategies that one uses when encountering a text. Third, they are very concerned that reading has both long- and short-term effects. Finally, challengers view reading inappropriate material as an inevitable "slippery slope" to poor moral character and behavior.

Books as a Legitimating Medium

Throughout challengers' discourse there is an emphasis on the process of legitimation within the marketplace of ideas. When an idea or concept is published it then becomes a legitimate idea or concept and it is through the act of writing and circulation that ideas gain traction in society. Writing and publishing are powerful actions for challengers. Since the book is a legitimating medium, authors and publishers must be careful to use their power wisely.[16] For challengers, books can change the course of one's life and it is up to the people who create books to ensure that inappropriate materials are not circulated in the wider public.

In the discourse of challengers, the process of writing and publishing what they consider to be immoral ideas is seen as inherently destructive. As demonstrated above, challengers are often surprised that someone would bother to write or publish the materials that they are challenging. They place great emphasis on the selection process of publication. If an author sends in a work riddled with vulgarity or sexuality, then it is the duty of publishers not to publish the manuscript. This is vitally important because once something is published and in the marketplace of ideas it has the legitimacy of having been published and printed in a book—an act that affords it authority and increases its power. If this selection process fails, then the institution has a duty not to buy it because this legitimacy cannot be removed from the work and, for challengers, the only perceived recourse is to remove or relocate the book.

Commonsense and the Imagination

Not only are books a legitimating medium, they are also, unlike film or television, an unmediated medium. There are no outside entities between the reader and the text. As noted previously, books, unlike broadcast television or movies, are somewhat difficult to censor once acquired by the reader. This lack of mediation informs the interpretive strategies that are discussed throughout challengers' discourse.

Commonsense interpretation of text is the primary interpretive strategy that informs challengers' discourse. This is the idea that the words in text mean what they say and there is little recourse to different methods of interpretation. Of particular importance is the understanding of the nature of truth in texts. Since texts are subject to commonsense interpretation, when an author states something in writing, it must be true. For challengers, truth telling is a vital component of both fiction and nonfiction. Being "made up" is not an excuse for not telling the "truth" in texts. Truth here includes proper consequences for characters' immoral behavior within the text itself. Without these outcomes, books cannot be proper instructional material.

Along with commonsense interpretation, the work of imagination is an important aspect of understanding how challengers construct the practice of reading. When one reads, one visualizes what is happening on the page, and it is this visualization that most concerns challengers. There are certain situations and behaviors that those who possess an undisciplined imagination, that is, children, should not encounter. Children, in particular, lack critical distance from texts, and reading inappropriate materials will lead them to have unsuitable reactions to such materials.

Short- and Long-Term Effects of Reading

Commonsense interpretation and the imagination are also connected to the idea of reading effects. Because there is little room for polysemy and reading is a powerful practice, the effects of reading are viewed as inevitable for challengers. Reading inappropriate material when one is a child will inexorably lead to both long- and short-term outcomes. In the short term, challengers are especially concerned with how the imagination affects children physically and emotionally. Physical responses to text, such as sexual excitement and violence, are common references throughout their discourse. It must be noted that both of these are seen as both negative and inevitable and reading the inappropriate material will lead inescapably to behavior that is considered to be immoral because children, by their nature, cannot process the material. Feelings of embarrassment and hurt are used as proxies for identifying objectionable books. If a child experiences hurt or embarrassment while reading, then the text is inappropriate by definition.

Long-term effects of reading inappropriate material include the degradation and corrosion of the soul and/or the development of poor moral character. This particular interpretive strategy is not surprising since challengers place so much faith in the power of reading. If your life can change by reading a book on environmentalism, the Bible, or *Das Kapital*, how could it not change when reading a book that tells a story about sexual violence? It is not hyperbole to state that some challengers argue that one's basic character is put in play when reading. This is why it is vital that only "good" materials are presented to children. The concept that all texts are read in the same way and therefore must induce physical and emotional effects is key to understanding the actions of challengers.

Causal Arguments

The argument that the effects of reading justify the censorship of books is similar to feminist arguments against pornography and has parallels to "slippery slope" arguments used in antidrug campaigns. Just as smoking cigarettes or marijuana is a gateway to using harder drugs, reading inappropriate material is a gateway to exhibiting poor behavior. If children see that certain behaviors are legitimized by their inclusion in books that are then sanctioned by the public library or school, they will believe that such behaviors are correct.

As with antipornography arguments, reading about a particular behavior legitimizes it and leads to worse behavior in the reader later in life. In some respects, the challenged books are not simply like pornography—they are pornography. Since the texts lead the reader to visualize sexual or violent acts, the challenged books cannot be classified as literature. The inclusion of such acts in the challenged texts means that they cannot have permanent, enduring value in the same way that literature does.

These four themes concerning reading and the book constitute a particular conceptualization of print culture for challengers. Their discourse focuses on the book as a legitimating symbolic object within the marketplace of ideas and the effects of reading in order to justify the action of removing or relocating objectionable material within public institutions. Although these arguments are not necessarily unique to challengers, the actions that they are meant to justify are distinctive. However, it must be noted that challengers are only sometimes successful in their endeavors and the outcome of their cases often rests in the hands of librarians and other staff and administrators in public schools and libraries who wield significant symbolic power within their institutions.

The following chapter uses a slightly different lens to analyze challengers' discourse than the one found in this and the previous chapter. First, instead of focusing on what challengers say, it focuses on how they say it. In particular, it explores challengers' use of martial language and the sense that they are an embattled minority engaged in spiritual warfare. Second, the chapter explores in more detail the remedies that challengers suggest to assuage their fears regarding objectionable materials in public institutions.

NOTES

1. Eric Gonzales, "Meridian Police Show Up to Free Book Giveaway," *KBOI 2 News*, April 23, 2014, accessed May 12, 2014, http://www.kboi2.com/news/local/Meridian-police-show-up-to-free-book-giveaway--256475781.html.

2. Tom Boggioni, "Concerned Idaho Citizen Calls Police over Public Banned Book Giveaway to High School Students," *Raw Story*, April 27, 2014, accessed May 15, 2014, http://www.rawstory.com/rs/2014/04/27/concerned-idaho-citizen-calls-police-over-public-banned-book-giveaway-to-high-school-students/; Doktor Zoom, "Derp Roundup: Idaho Parents Call Cops to Protect Children from Banned Book," *Wonkette*, April 26, 2014, accessed May 12, 2014, http://wonkette.com/547677/derp-roundup-idaho-parents-call-cops-to-protect-children-from-banned-book#K3LderIEXU4AHUPO.99.

3. Bill Roberts, "The Absolutely True Story of What Happened to That Book in Meridian," *Idaho Statesman*, April 2, 2014, accessed May 12, 2014, http://www.idahostatesman.com/2014/04/02/3114247/the-absolutely-true-story-of-what.html.

4. Gonzales, "Meridian Police Show Up."

5. Although it is not scholarly, the best description of the term "edify" can be found on the blog *Stuff Christian Culture Likes* at http://www.stuffchristianculturelikes.com/2011/05/blog-post.html.

6. Daniel Selcer, *Philosophy and the Book: Early Modern Figures of Material Inscription* (New York: Continuum, 2010), 192.

7. George Marsden, *Understanding Fundamentalism and Evangelicalism* (Grand Rapids, MI: Eerdmans, 1991), 157.

8. In his article on the reception and interpretation of the *Left Behind* novels by evangelicals, Paul Gutjahr discusses the long-held ambivalence with which American Protestants viewed the popular novel. American Christians gradually accepted Christian fiction, but it is clear that this acceptance was not all-encompassing. Their views on other types of fiction are still somewhat negative. Gutjahr writes that "as late as 1993, one irate Protestant author . . . titled a pleading article that appeared in the major protestant periodical *Christianity Today* 'Stop Rejecting Fiction!'" (p. 210). It is possible that the phrase "garbage in, garbage out" is related to this ambivalence toward fiction. Paul C. Gutjahr, "No Longer Left Behind: Amazon.Com, Reader Response, and the Changing Fortunes of the Christian Novel in America," *Book History*, 2002, 209–36.

9. Katie Roiphe, "It Was, Like, All Dark and Stormy," *Wall Street Journal*, June 6, 2009, sec. News, http://online.wsj.com/news/articles/SB10001424052970203771904574173403357573642.

10. Alexie, Sherman. *The absolutely true diary of a part-time Indian*. New York, NY: Little, Brown, 2007.

11. I am not arguing here that only challengers believe that reading has effects. However, it is significant that challengers believe that the effects of reading are inevitable and that there is a correlation between what one reads and how one behaves. This is in contrast to the view in modern librarianship, which is agnostic to the effects of reading material. According to this viewpoint, since it is impossible to know the effects of reading a particular text, one can be open to keeping all points of view within a collection. See Emily J. M. Knox, "Intellectual Freedom and the Agnostic-Postmodern View of Reading Effects," *Library Trends* 63, no. 1 (2014).

12. Although it did not become one of the cases used in this study, two statements from one of the pilot interviews that I conducted encapsulate the discourse used in challenge cases and were instructive for analyzing the discourse of challengers, especially concerning reading effects. Cathy's [pseudonym] interview was quite brief but her answers to the questions were direct. When I asked why she found the challenged material inappropriate she answered, "I would guess that it would have been sexual content. Because those are the things that I find most offensive. When there is something in a magazine that is sexually explicit or suggestive and I don't think it's appropriate for the age or I don't think it's something that should be paid for by tax money, then I don't feel comfortable with that."

Later in the interview, after being asked what she thought the effects of reading such material might be, Cathy stated, "I just think that when you have children or anyone who might be sexually aroused by sexually explicit material and that is not a behavior that you want in young children or young teens. Then I don't see that as a healthy environment for them."

Although many of the challengers throughout the case did not use the same blunt language as Cathy, their arguments echo her concerns.

13. This argument was first put forward by Andrea Dworkin and Catharine A. MacKinnon in *Pornography and Civil Rights: A New Day for Women's Equality* (Minneapolis, MN: Organizing Against Pornography, 1988), and it is a major theme in second-wave feminist thought. That it is used by challengers in their own discourse demonstrates how this argument has permeated contemporary American society.

14. Note that I have no evidence that the challengers in this case in particular worked together and I cannot account for the similarity in their discourse.

15. It is possible that this is the speaker at the hearing in the statement above.

16. In some respects, this argument is not much different from the ones made regarding scholarly publishing. Academics and librarians place great trust in scholarly publishers to weed through illegitimate information. Once a work has been published, it has the imprimatur of the publisher and is considered to be a legitimate piece of scholarly writing.

Chapter Six

Fear, Knowledge, and Power

BOUNDARIES AND VALUES IN THE COMMUNITY

Like most academics, when people ask what I study I have a short elevator speech prepared. Mine is something like this: "I study people who try to ban books in public libraries and schools." The responses that I receive to this short speech are varied. Some people tell me about recent book challenges that they have heard about in the news while others respond, "Does that still happen?" It is the latter response that is most interesting to me. It seems that when many people think about "banning" books they imagine it is something that took place in the past. Often a follow-up question centers on the perceived futility of what book challengers are trying to accomplish—"But you can get books everywhere!" I am often told. This response illuminates the question that this book is attempting to answer: What is the point of banning books and what are book challengers trying to accomplish in our age of ubiquitous access?[1] As I have noted throughout this study, in order to understand the actions of challengers it is necessary to look beyond challengers' actions into the justifications that they give through their discourse regarding the symbolic role of books in public institutions. Overall, I believe that their discourse shows that challengers are engaged in symbolic action when they attempt to remove, relocate, or restrict an objectionable book from the school curriculum, media center, or public library shelves. They are making a statement about their society, their community, and their personal values through these actions.

More specifically, book challengers are attempting to both make a statement and effect change within their communities' institutions through their actions; namely, they are trying to ensure that these institutions reflect their own values. Although this may seem somewhat obvious, it is a point that is

121

often lost in the media coverage and general umbrage that tends to accompany book challenges. Challengers use their symbolic capital and power within the community as citizens, parents, and taxpayers to effect these changes. Note that challengers do not argue that no one should have access to the knowledge contained in these books but that their own communities' institutions should not provide this access to, in the cases studied here, the children and youth that reside in these communities. That is, for the challengers, the values that are espoused in a particular community via the symbols of its library collections or public school curricula should be in keeping with the challengers' own value system. This is coupled with an unyielding viewpoint regarding how exposure to knowledge affects the reader. Although there are various reasons why particular texts are targeted, including sexual content, violence, and stereotyping, challengers share a worldview regarding the effect of this difficult and objectionable knowledge on those who will read it. They also argue that the outcomes will be negative for the reader, community, and society at large. Within challengers' discourse, there is a particular sense of fear that American society is rapidly changing and it is up to the challengers and our shared institutions to protect children from some of the less desirable aspects of these changes.

This final chapter provides an analysis of the language of challengers' discourse and the remedies that they suggest, as well as a short summary of some of the themes discussed throughout the study. It begins by looking at how a sense of fear and anxiety is constructed in challengers' discourse by focusing on their use of the language of spiritual warfare and their feelings of being an embattled minority. Then, it focuses on two possible actions that challengers offer as remedies for the inclusion of problematic material in public institutions: the use of permission slips and labeling. Finally, the chapter offers some concluding remarks regarding the attempts to remove, restrict, and relocate books within public institutions.

ON THE RIGHT SIDE OF HISTORY

Instead of focusing on the explicit reasoning that challengers give for their actions, which was the primary focus of the previous two chapters, this section discusses how challengers view themselves. As will be demonstrated below, challengers often argue that they are fighting against the majority of people in American society who hold values that are different from their own. This positioning is exemplified through their use of language of war and aggression, which has a distinctively apocalyptic tone.

An Embattled Minority

Throughout challengers' discourse there is a prevailing sense that they are one of the few individuals left on the side of "morality." They are willing to speak up in their community for what they believe is right even in the face of opposition from many of their neighbors:[2]

> So don't tell me that this is preparing our kids, ok. Because that's not accept-able to me. And it's not acceptable to people—a lot of people. But because we're standing up and saying "No, this is wrong" and we may be the minority today—that does not mean we're wrong. It just means we have the guts to stand up for our kids and children. And I don't want my grandchildren and I don't want your 3-year-olds to be told that this is acceptable in our society. It doesn't work that way. (Male speaker #3, Book challenge hearing, Clark-stown, NY, March 24, 2011)

The speaker quoted above states that, because of his willingness to ask that a book be removed, he is demonstrating a bravery that other community members do not possess. He is willing to accept the ire of his neighbors in order to protect both his and other people's children and grandchildren. For him, it is more important to be "right" than for others to agree with him.

Another challenger in Stockton, Missouri, uses the dwindling rates of religious believers as a framework for discussing his sense of being one of the few who adhere to a particular set of beliefs:

> I am actually here as a Christian. . . . It's estimated in sources from campus ministries that 75% of practicing Christians fall away from the Christian faith during their first year of college. Abortion rates among Christians and post-Christians are the same as others. Divorce rates are at parity with unbelievers. Professing believers walk the same, dress the same, watch the same movies, and read the same books. We're living in a post-Christian culture partially caused by post-Modernism that says that all truth is relative and we live in a world where there is [no] absolute truth. (Male speaker #3, Book challenge hearing, Stockton, MO, September 8, 2010)

Not only is he a minority in his community, this speaker feels that he is a minority even among his fellow Christians. There are no delineating characteristics or behavior markers between Christians and "post-Christians." His statement implies that the book in question should not be read by Christians but since everyone reads "the same books" such material is considered to be acceptable by all, including those who call themselves Christians.

The challenger in Lewiston, Maine, also makes an explicit claim that her stance on the challenged book makes her part of a dwindling minority:

> The greatest war against human civilization is immorality. History will look back on the past 30–50 years as a dark time in human civilization. I felt a great

sense of sadness when I received your e-mail. I keep hoping there might be a
remnant with a dutiful sense of responsibility towards the youth. (Letter to the
board, Lewiston, ME, August 20, 2007)

In this statement she explicitly links the perceived moral decline of the nation, as discussed in chapter 4, with the idea that she is on the losing side of
the battle. Of particular interest is her use of the term "remnant." The "remnant," or the faithful few who are left after the apocalypse, is a common
theme throughout the apocalyptic and spiritual warfare literature.[3] It is clear
that, for this challenger, there are only a few left in society who are willing to
battle against immorality.

The Language of Spiritual Warfare

As noted previously, challengers use apocalyptic language with a distinctively militaristic tone. Although it is often assumed that challengers are religious conservatives, this is not always the case, and this study included challengers who targeted books for nonreligious reasons. However, the language
of spiritual warfare is a distinctive characteristic across challengers' discourse. This language, although often based in religious worldviews is not
necessarily related to theology. That is, the language is often used to describe
changes in the secular realm.[4] Challengers also speak of society falling into
"rebellion" and carrying out "assaults" on decency. Another discusses a
"war" on human civilization. One speaker at the Stockton, Missouri, public
hearing plainly notes that

> civilization has indeed failed. They flourish depending on how moral that
> civilization is. A civilization is a group of people who are civil along with
> cultural refinement, along with infrastructure, and civilizations fail in direct
> proportion to corruption. Then there's God. Some people like to give him a
> name that we can't repeat in the pledge of allegiance. A name that we're going
> to chase out of the public square. A person—and he is a person, not just a
> spirit. We're created in his image. And some would have us not even allow us
> to give him thanks in a public school. (Male speaker #5, Book challenge
> hearing, Stockton, MO, September 8, 2010)

The speaker's definition of civilization is clear: A civilization is a moral,
culturally refined society with a robust infrastructure whose people eschew
corruption. Of particular interest is the explicit link the challenger makes
between morality and civilization as well as the implicit understanding that
the presence of a particular book symbolizes the failure of civilization. The
challenged book's availability in the Stockton School District demonstrates a
lack of "cultural refinement" and the failure of the district, through its purchase of the challenged book, to adhere to the parameters of the civilized
world. This is also a theme in a letter to the administration of the local public

library from the Lewiston, Maine, challenger in which she states that "the greatest war against human civilization is immorality" (Letter to the board, Lewiston, ME, August 20, 2007). It is clear from this language that challenges are not based simply on differences of opinion but are a struggle over what the moral structures of society will be in the future.

The themes of the moral drift of society, as discussed in chapter 4, are often strongly yoked with ideas concerning sexual morality and gender roles for many of the challengers' understanding of social and moral order. The structures of many challengers' worldviews in these areas tilt toward what one might call a traditional morality wherein the proper outlet for sexuality is within a heterosexual married, family unit.[5] The following letter writer from Clarkstown, New York, associates all three of the themes concerning society:

> My wife and I have a Judaio-Christian [*sic*] perspective which stands directly opposed to such worldliness. If one is to conclude that the basic building block of society is the family unit—and that traditionally Is [*sic*] understood as one man, one woman, and their offspring, then to propose any curriculum in the school system contrary to that, is to establish the society of the chaotic. There is a beautiful design and balance in the family unit as understood by my description. Within the construct of family design are limits and guidelines for behavior. One is not free in a moral society to act immorally without consequences. The designers of our constitution realized this. Without an established set of moral codes and guidelines, once again, chaos is the end result and the destruction of such a society. (Request for reconsideration #1, Clarkstown, NY, date redacted [February 2011])

The letter writer and his wife are "directly opposed" to the "worldliness" of the larger society. "Chaos" and "destruction" will prevail if the school system does not support a traditionally organized society. Of particular importance for him and other challengers is the role of the family and the support it receives from public institutions within the public sphere: the family and particularly parents play an important role in setting boundaries for their children in order to save them from the "society of the chaotic" and "worldliness."

However, it should be noted that such traditional views are not always part of the challengers' worldviews. Although challengers are often conservative Christians, there are also many challenges for more progressive reasons. For example, one challenger in this study was concerned with use of bigoted language in *Brave New World* to describe Native Americans while another challenger was concerned with the depiction of violence in the book *Stolen Children*. Another challenger, in Greensboro, North Carolina, was concerned about many aspects of Walter Dean Myers's book *Hoops* but the use of the term "nigger" in particular:

Upon helping my son Matthew with his difficulties he was experiencing we immediately noticed that this book was full of derogatory remarks, violence towards females, profanity, offensive racial slurs, weapons referencing and sexual content. I also found that this book had been challenged and banned from schools nationwide for the exact same items that I was finding offensive.

Specifically there are two pages from this book that I wish to reference. Page 152–153 it states:

Page 152, paragraph 4 "They came to me and said 'Nigger, who you think you are?' They said, 'Ain't you that nigger that used to fix ball games in Chicago?'"

Page 153, paragraph 2 "I'm the nigger who sold his game."

Page 153, paragraph 6 "Brothers sitting in there feeling on their dreams like they [are] masturbating."

These quotes are just a few of the offensive writings in this book. We have also attached copies of pages from this book that contains [offensive] language. (Request for reconsideration, Greensboro, NC, November 8, 2010)

It is important to note that even in these cases, the challengers still made arguments concerning the spiritual welfare of children and the effects of reading. That is, the argument that censorship is justified when it comes to certain types of knowledge is not simply an argument on the right. It is an argument that centers on difficult knowledge (which might be, for example, the idea that famous authors equate Native Americans with savages) and access to this knowledge within books. Regardless of the reasons given for removing, restricting, or relocating a particular book, almost all challengers argue that public institutions must draw boundaries regarding certain types of knowledge. One method that institutions might use to accomplish this is to implement a system of permissions and standards.

PERMISSIONS AND STANDARDS

Permission Slips

Encouraging the use of permission slips as a policy is a common theme in challengers' discourse. Permission slips operate as a type of boundary object in these cases. "Boundary objects" are defined as forms and other written communication documents required by the challenge process. These include the requests for reconsideration that are initially filed by challengers as well as the policy documents approved and publicly published by governing bodies. Boundary objects allow for communication across various information contexts and social objects. As Geoffrey C. Bowker and Susan Leigh Star note, boundary objects "inhabit several communities of practice and satisfy the information requirements of each of them."[6] This study demonstrates that challengers do not always view these objects, such as the request for reconsideration forms, in a positive light, and staff and administrators in public institutions often use boundary objects to mitigate the voices of outsiders. A challenger in Merrill, Wisconsin, notes that the public library requires children under the age of 18 to have parents' permission to check out a particular book. It is an official document that allows for communication between the institution and the parent. Note that the use of permission slips is highly unusual in a public library setting and against the Library Code of Ethics.[7] However, the challenger is arguing that the fact that the book requires permission to be read in the public library is sufficient reasoning for removing the book from the high school curriculum:

> [He] just said to get it out of the public library you have to sign it out to the parents if they're under 18 to check it out and they get it out of the high school library without problem. That seems to be a little odd. It's in the adult section of the public library. We don't have an adult section in the high school library. They have it in there because they said there's explicit material in it that has to do with pedophilia and suicide. (Male speaker #1, Book challenge hearing, Merrill, WI, September 29, 2011)

In this case the public library's policies are used as a justification for removing a book from the school library. Note that the issue of various sections as well as the physical layout of the library is prominent in the challenger's statement. Since it lacks an adult section, the school library must only contain material that is appropriate for children.[8]

In a similar vein to the challenger above, another challenger in Merrill, Wisconsin, suggests using technology to indicate whether or not children are permitted to check out a particular book. She discusses alternative policies for the book in the library and the classroom:

> I do believe if we leave it in the library it should be under a situation where the parents can log in as Mr. [Redacted] suggested and issue their opinion on whether or not they would like their child to take the book out. I would not have a problem with this being in place and that this could be something that could be a choice to do a book report on. As long as another student has the right to choose their own book as well. (Female speaker #11, Book challenge hearing, Merrill, WI, September 29, 2011)

It is important to note that using technology in the manner suggested by this challenger would be against the Library Code of Ethics. Like many challengers, this speaker is concerned that the school would be acting against the will of parents if it allowed children to check out a particular book without their parents' permission. As described in chapter 4, the theme of parents as boundary setters with regard to the media consumption of their children is an important one in challengers' discourse.

In another curriculum challenge, parents were required to fill out a permission slip prior to their children reading a particular book. However, many of the challengers felt that the permission slip did not adequately convey the controversial nature of material in the book. As one challenger remarks:

> The English Department has grossly misrepresented this book to parents. Their permission slip is vague and white-washed. We truly believe if all parents were able to see the graphic excerpts of this book, most would not allow their child to read it. (Request for reconsideration #1, Clarkstown, NY, date redacted [February 2011])

The permission slip did not sufficiently elucidate the inappropriate material in the book. For the challenger, it is an inadequate boundary object since it did not fulfill its duty to communicate information between different information contexts and settings. Without adequate information regarding the book, the challenger argues that parents could not make an informed decision regarding whether or not their children should read the book.

Parallels among various procedures used by libraries and schools are a common theme in challengers' discourse. The school in Merrill, Wisconsin, required parents to sign an Internet usage form for their children, and one challenger notes that she thought that the same guidelines would be used for library books in the school:

> I find that was a phenomenal document for us to sign so we can protect [our] children. The parents sign that and the children sign that, and everybody signs it. I thought this was a wonderful document. And what I thought was that . . . I was under the impression that with all of the material in our school district, this was also followed when you would [pick] things out. All of our material in our school district would follow this type of a guideline. So you can imagine my shock when I did see that in a book, this book *Montana 1948*. I thought our diligence for the other material was followed. I just thought that. But when I found that book, I totally 100% lost my trust. I felt the contract for my internet usage was broken by our school district and that's not a good thing. (Female speaker #6, Book challenge hearing, Merrill, WI, September 29, 2011)

Here the permission slip for Internet use is described as a "phenomenal document" that adequately fulfills its role as a boundary object. For this challenger, the challenged book is not in line with the standards required by the school for Internet use. Therefore she does not understand how the item could be included in the curriculum when students would not be able to view what she believes to be similar material on the Internet.

Labeling and Standards

Another common theme throughout challengers' discourse concerns the use of labels to alert parents to the presence of objectionable material in public and school library collections. Labels, like movie ratings discussed in a previous chapter, are markers that allow individuals to immediately categorize a particular object. They are also performative. For example, if a book is labeled as "romance," one is able to recognize the text as part of a particular genre that follows certain writing conventions. The book also becomes a "romance" as opposed to fantasy or some other genre. As one letter writer states:

> It is perfectly dishonorable that public libraries have no warnings of the pornographic materials on the shelves in the children's section. The book teaches the children how to have sex and is a predator's dream come true. . . . It is a truly disordered concept of freedom when library policies adopt children's capability to get pornographic material. (Letter to the board, Lewiston, ME, August 20, 2007)

The use of the term "pornographic" demonstrates that this challenger disapproves of the lack of warning labels on public library books. Since the books in public libraries do not have labels, the challenger is not able to immediately recognize which books might contain objectionable material and the space is disordered and unsafe. That is, there is no structuring structure in place for recognizing inappropriate materials in the library. The challenger argues that library administrators, by failing to label objectionable books, therefore support policies that are harmful to children and youth. Note that labeling materials, like the use of permission slips, is also against the Library Code of Ethics. Although librarians may label materials as directional aids, these must be value neutral. The use of prejudicial labels is discoursed. These are labels intended to "restrict access based on a value judgment that the content, language, or themes of the material or the background or views of the creator(s) of the material, render it inappropriate or offensive for all or certain groups of users."[9]

It is not surprising that the Motion Picture Association of America's (MPAA) rating system is often described by challengers as a model that libraries and schools can adopt to help parents find "appropriate" materials for their children. The MPAA's system offers parents a marker regarding the content of a particular movie, and many parents use the ratings as a benchmark for determining whether or not their children may watch a movie. The presence of the ratings system creates a sense of order and safety with regard to movies. As one challenger states:

> For people who want this book, they can ask for it, the book is available. Go buy it. Get it online. I didn't let my kids when they were five watch R-rated movies for the same reasons. You need to draw a line as to what is appropriate and what's not. If other parents want to provide other information to their kids. Fine. It's up to them. But I don't think we need to have it in the public schools. (Male speaker #5, Book challenge hearing, Bedford, NH, February 28, 2011)

More surprising is the argument by analogy comparing the labeling of books to the actions of standards and practices departments found in print and broadcast media. Standards and practices departments ensure that publications and shows adhere to the broadcaster's or publisher's own standards regarding obscenity, violence, and sexuality. [10] As the challenger in Lewiston, Maine, notes, none of the print or broadcast media she contacted showed pictures from the book she is challenging:

> Why is it that the newspapers and television stations I have been in contact with since August of this year neither print nor show the illustrations and Writings of "I P N?" One television station told me they would be sued by the Federal Communications Commission if they showed the contents of the book in question. What a contradiction that is when youth of any age can easily remove for their perusal this book without restrictions. What a contradiction when L P L has recently increased to ten more books of "I P N" to be on its shelf violating City of Lewiston's Obscenity Codes and still the printed and television media are restricted to view what children easily can get their hands on at L P L. (Letter to the board, Lewiston, ME, August 20, 2007)

The standards and practices of print publishers and broadcasters also operate as a structuring structure that allows individuals to recognize and categorize materials in newspapers and on broadcast television as "safe" for consumption. If the materials are perceived to be inappropriate for these outlets, which follow particular standards for content, then, challengers argue, they are also inappropriate for the library. This challenger sets up an opposition between the library and media outlets. Why is the library willing to violate standards when the local television station is not willing to go that far? The television station's actions provide all the evidence that is needed to prove that the public library is acting irresponsibly and in a manner that violates commonly held standards. For this challenger, the public library, by collecting books such as *It's Perfectly Normal*, is even in violation of the town's own obscenity codes. Therefore, the institution has taken a position that does not correlate with how the challenger structures "libraries" in her worldview.

The interviewee from Helena, Montana, also mentions broadcasting and publishing standards:

> For the same reasons when I spoke publically in the meeting about it the press was there but I knew they wouldn't print what I . . . I recited the same passages as I did to you. They would not print that because the media has standards. You would never hear this kind of language on TV. On CNN. Or in the newspapers. They have standards. So it is . . . isn't it interesting. They allow the kids to read it. But they could not speak it out loud. (Interview with challenger, Helena, MT, December 12, 2011)

This challenger implies that the library should follow the same standards as the media. Note that these challengers do not question why the library might have these different practices in place. For them, the broadcast media and libraries are structured in the same way and they are spaces that must protect children. The broadcast media is regarded as doing a better job of protecting children by adhering to standards that do not allow objectionable material to be consumed by minors.

Classroom standards are also viewed by challengers as a model that libraries can follow. Of particular interest are arguments concerning how controversial material will be discussed in the classroom:

> It's so bad that they couldn't discuss it in the classroom. Because the classroom has standards. Teachers, staff have standards. The way they speak . . . the way they conduct themselves. And so they couldn't talk about the book in the classroom. All those parts because they weren't up to standard. But it was okay for the children to read. (Interview with challenger, Helena, MT, December 12, 2011)

If the information in a particular book is too controversial to be discussed in a classroom, then, challengers argue, why should the book be included in the library? The relationship between the appropriateness of a book and its suitability for discussion was discussed in more detail in the previous chapter. Here it is important to note that challengers argue that the standards in the classroom correspond to those used in the library. Another challenger in Merrill, Wisconsin, also discusses the idea that the school is not adhering to its own standards when objectionable material is allowed in the curriculum or library. "Our" refers to guidelines from the school administration:

> My concern is not just this book, but how much has been allowed into the school that goes against our own guidelines? My ultimate question is who are all the individuals supporting this material in our school and then holding them accountable for their actions. (Request for reconsideration, Merrill, WI, June 15, 2011)

For this challenger, the presence of the book is a symbol of declining standards in the whole school. Although the challenger is using the challenge process to remove this particular book, he or she is most concerned that whoever is in charge be held accountable for allowing such a book into the school in order to ensure that it does not happen again.

The public library and school are vital parts of the local community for challengers. They both represent the community to the wider world and shape the values and morals of the next generation. As noted in chapter 2, they are embodiments of the conversion of economic capital into symbolic capital. As symbolic objects, community-supported public institutions provide a particular image of the community to the wider society and it is this, as well as the sense that these institutions must be a place of safety, that so concerns challengers.

A WORLDVIEW OF DESTRUCTION AND INNOCENCE

Book challenges represent the movement of a private act (determining what one's own children should read) into the public sphere. This movement is based in challengers' particular understanding of what the public sphere is and how it operates. For them, this social sphere is a symbolic representation of community values and beliefs. Since they are supported by the community and—in some respects—are the public face of the community to the wider society, institutions within the public sphere should only contain carefully selected, ordered knowledge.

Challengers' worldviews are quite complex, but there are several common themes found throughout their discourse that relate to the overall ordering of social space. In particular, challengers share particular conceptualizations of society, parenting, and the nature of childhood. Society is viewed as a fragile backbone that is under attack from immoral forces while parenting is considered to be an important, boundary-setting role within the social moral order. Finally, children are constructed as innocents whose status must be preserved at all costs.

A Fragile Society

For challengers, society is structured as a backbone for life, but it is one that is quite fragile and will shatter if individuals do not adhere to certain values and morals. It is, in its most basic form, a structuring structure for challengers. American society has altered dramatically in the past 50 years, and challengers view these changes with trepidation. In fact, for many challengers, these changes have sent American society on a course of destruction that needs to be reversed. Shifts in sexual mores and gender roles as well as the perception of pervasive vulgarity and violence throughout the media landscape are leading society, according to their discourse, on a path to destruction.

The objectionable materials that are the object of challenges are constructed by challengers as both a symptom of these changes and a symbol of them: if the shifts in society had not taken place, then objectionable material would not have been written or published in books, much less be available in public institutions in the first place. At the same time, the books—with their pervasive sexuality, violence, stereotyping, or other harmful material—represent the shifts themselves to challengers. According to the challengers' discourse, the assaults on society have been especially taxing for the nuclear family, and parenting, in particular, has become more challenging.

Parenting and Boundaries

The family unit is one of the primary structures of society for challengers, and throughout their discourse they describe changes to the family unit—outcomes of the social upheavals of the '60s—in apocalyptic terms. Parenting is perceived by challengers to be both "natural" and difficult. It is natural because one should automatically know to set boundaries regarding media consumption for one's children. At the same time, parenting is also difficult because there are so many forces working against parents who, for example, attempt to set strict boundaries for their children.

The idea of parent as boundary setter is pervasive in challengers' discourse. This is often described by challengers using a causal argument: if parents set clear boundaries, then their children will develop into morally sound adults. According to challengers, however, some parents are unable or unwilling to set such boundaries. These parents are "falling down on the job" and it is the duty of public schools and libraries to support them—and all parents—in their difficult role. For challengers, selecting objectionable material makes parenting harder, and public institutions must help all parents set adequate boundaries for children by removing or relocating such materials. This charge to public institutions becomes even more important for challengers when they consider parents who are not fulfilling their roles as boundary setters and therefore compromising their children's innocence. Challengers present themselves as monitors for public institutions who will prevent all children from encountering objectionable material, even if other parents are unable or unwilling to do so.

Innocence and Childhood

Throughout their discourse, challengers view childhood in two different ways. The first view constructs innocence as a state of ignorance. That is, children are a tabula rasa and do not have any knowledge of sexuality, vulgarity, or violence. Challengers who hold this first view describe these characteristics as learned behaviors that only become a part of someone's character if he or she is exposed to them at an early age. The second conceptualization of childhood innocence found in challengers' discourse holds that characteristics such as sexuality, vulgarity, and violence are innate and latent. In this view, all human beings have aspects of these behaviors as part of their nature, but they only manifest themselves through exposure to material that contains sexuality, vulgarity, or violence. That is, one might become violent if one is exposed to texts or images that contain violence. If not exposed to such material, the trait remains dormant.

Regardless of how it is constructed, challengers view innocence as something that must be protected and the challenged material is seen as an assault on this inherent trait. Protection from objectionable materials is also linked to challengers' conceptualization of parents as boundary setters. By setting boundaries and attempting to remove or relocate materials in public institutions, parents maintain their children's innocence.

Print Culture and Reading Practices

As noted in chapter 2, reading is neither a single action nor a solitary activity that is fixed across space and time but a constructed social practice. The act of "reading" a text can mean that one is reading aloud to others or reading silently or even listening to an audiobook. The strategies used to interpret the text have also changed over time. For example, medieval reading practices often focused on the "fourfold senses," while today there is more of an emphasis on the critical distance of the reader from the text.

This study demonstrates that many of the people who challenge books conceptualize reading similarly. For them, reading is a powerful activity that can change a person's life and guide an individual on the correct path, or it can destroy that individual's character. Challengers often have great respect for books as symbolic, material objects and it is imperative that the texts contained within them contain information that "edifies" the soul.

The Book as Revered Object

As noted above, challengers consider reading to be a powerful activity and some of this influence is rooted in the symbolic power of the book itself. This symbolic authority operates in two ways: First, the book is a powerful medium because it is an authoritative object within the marketplace of ideas. Second, challengers argue that the presence of a particular text within a book confers legitimacy upon the text. These two conceptualizations of the power of the book are self-perpetuating: the book confers legitimacy to the text, which increases the symbolic values of the book, which confers legitimacy to the text.

This reverence for the book is clear throughout challengers' discourse. One result of this reverence is that they rarely suggest defacing or burning the books they are challenging. Instead, they argue that people who create books, authors and publishers, should themselves be aware of the power of books and not allow inappropriate concepts and ideas to be included in them. That is, because a book is such a powerful object, those who create them should do everything in their power to keep "bad" ideas from receiving the legitimacy afforded by the book. Once a text is published, it is too late for the ideas to be withdrawn from the marketplace and it is incumbent upon the reader to have the skills to correctly interpret and respond to the text or the text should be withdrawn or relocated.

Mimetic Interpretive Strategies

There are two prominent interpretive strategies described in challengers' discourse. The first concerns the mimetic characteristics of the immature imagination. For many challengers, children and youth simply lack the maturity (that is, to use Davidson's terms, possess an undisciplined imagination) to have distance from a text. Therefore, when they read, texts are translated not simply into images but also experiences. For challengers, reading is an experiential activity—the reader goes through the same events as the narrator or protagonist. This means that reading about inappropriate behavior can lead directly to inappropriate behavior in one's life. Challengers argue that there is little to no distance between the immature reader and the text.

Another interpretive strategy that challengers discuss concerns the nature of truth and its relationship to text. This is intimately tied to the reverence for the book described above as well as the idea that reading should edify the soul. Since the presence of text in a book confers legitimacy, the text must also be "true." For challengers, this often means that the voice of the narrator or protagonist must contain only factual truths in fictional texts. There is little room for polysemic interpretation or even unreliable narrators in challengers' worldviews. The words in the text are what the author means. Challengers' discourse makes little distinction between fiction and nonfiction and all texts must be factually true, even if it is in the voice of a character in a novel. This practice of reading is based in a commonsense interpretive strategy of the text, wherein the text is exactly as it appears and the truth of the text is directly related to the effects of reading on individual behavior.

The Effects of Reading

Challengers often argue that reading texts that contain "bad" ideas or values can lead to both short- and long-term harmful effects in children. As noted above, challengers' discourse focuses on reading as a mimetic activity and therefore reading such material will result in damaging behavior. For example, with regard to short-term effects, some challengers argue that children who have been victims of sexual abuse or violence reexperience their trauma when they read a text that contains such events. Other challengers argue that reading about stereotypes will lead to children being hurt or embarrassed as a result of reading such texts.[11]

In regard to the practice of reading's long-term effects, challengers contend that children who read inappropriate material will turn out to have poor moral character. This argument is directly related to the power of reading wherein it is never considered to be an innocuous activity but one that challengers describe as having direct effects on one's character and behavior. This causal argument is crucial to understanding both challengers' worldviews and their arguments for removing and relocating books in public institutions.

Challengers employ the language of spiritual warfare in their discourse, demonstrating the peril in which they believe both the character and soul of the reader will be in if the reader is exposed to the objectionable media. They also propose two remedies that public institutions might use to assuage their fears: permission slips and labeling. Their view of the books sets them on a path to a particular action—one in which intervention is needed to save both the innocence of children and youth and the overall trajectory of society.

SYMBOLIC ACTION AND THE DISCOURSE OF CENSORSHIP

This study argues that the concept of worldview provides the best lens for understanding the discourse of censorship. It takes the arguments of challengers seriously and maintains that they are operating from a rational, systematic point of view that flows from their worldview. As noted in chapter 1, a worldview is defined as one's way of looking at the world that provides a road map for action. Worldviews consist of both how one perceives the world around oneself and how one projects meaning onto those perceptions. Although they consist of structured and structuring structures, worldviews are not necessarily coherent nor do they adhere to an ideal pattern. However, it is possible to build an image of worldviews by examining the repertoires individuals use in everyday life. For example, this study identifies particular aspects of challengers' worldviews including their understanding of society, public institutions, and reading practices. These aspects of challengers' worldviews aid our understanding of how challengers understand the world as well as their actions in bringing a challenge against a particular book.

Challengers' worldviews conceptualize the social space of society as a series of interlocking spheres that influence each other. Starting with the family, these spheres move outward to the community, then to the nation. Of significance for understanding challengers' worldviews is how deeply connected all these circles are with one another. The overall organization as well as institutions within one sphere has direct effects on the others. That is, the social upheavals of society directly affect both public institutions of the community and the institution of the nuclear family. This also operates in the opposite direction; according to challengers, what happens to the family has major implications for what happens in society.

Challengers' discourse often espouses this view at a highly symbolic level. As noted in the previous chapters, the presence of a particular book in a public institution is both a symptom and the cause of the destruction of society. For challengers, when a community "endorses" a particular book by having it in the curriculum or library shelves, this means both that the community itself has lost its standards and the community will continue to be unhealthy because it allows such inappropriate material. Without the remedy of removing or relocating the book, the community and therefore society will continue to decline. It is this issue of decline that most concerns challengers and characterizes much of the intensity found in the discourse of censorship. In order to protect society, the offending material must be removed or relocated. This is seen as one step that the local community can take to stave off the impending disaster. If the books are not removed or relocated, challengers argue, then the effects of allowing such objectionable ideas into the marketplace of ideas will first be felt by the children that challengers are trying to protect and then move outward into society.

It is the fear of these effects that leads directly to challengers' behavior. Challenging books is a method of relocating ambiguous materials within or removing anomalous material from public institutions that are part of the public marketplace of ideas within the public sphere. If the challenge is successful, order is restored and children and youth (as well as, by extension, society) will no longer be in danger in these institutions and the dire effects on society will no longer be a feared outcome. Challengers' discourse is primarily focused on staving off these effects.

As noted in chapter 1, this study analyzes both language and symbolic power. When challengers employ discourse to justify their actions, they are acting as *bricoleurs*. They pull from well-known and often well-respected discourses to argue that a particular type of knowledge should be removed from the public institutions. It is possible that these discourses are used because it is difficult to discuss censorship in modern society. The United States values "freedom" in a general sense as well as the First Amendment right to freedom of speech that is codified in the Constitution, and challengers are arguing that this freedom should be curbed for a certain group of people.

The discourse of censorship can be understood as a discourse of both anxiety and action. It focuses on the reasons why certain types of knowledge should not be made available to a particular population and is rooted in many different spheres. Challengers employ arguments from religious and scientific domains as well as a foundation regarding the power of books and reading. As noted in chapter 2, the commonsense interpretive strategy found throughout the discourse of censorship is rooted in both Common Sense philosophy and the concept of scientific Christianity, which views the Bible as a book of scientific facts. Challengers employ martial language, particular the terms "war" and "assault," to discuss the impending destruction of society. They also argue that institutions should employ ratings, labels, and permissions as remedies to the inclusion of difficult and forbidden knowledge on their shelves or in the curriculum. Although this study did not focus on the religious characteristics of challengers, Bible verses and stories appear throughout their discourse to bolster moral behavior and character. Causal or "slippery slope" arguments employed by challengers draw on scientific studies concerning the brain's development and the causes of "immoral" behavior as well as the idea that certain texts are a "gateway drug" to poor moral character. These discourses are combined by challengers to justify the removal or relocation of books in public institutions.

WANDING FOR WEAPONS

This book ends where it began—at another book challenge hearing—one that I did not get to attend but received a lot of media attention. This one is in Tucson, Arizona, and the picture below gives the reader a good idea of the atmosphere of the hearing. Before being let into the meeting, everyone was wanded for weapons including the nine-year-old boy in the picture below. Once again, this was a story with stark headlines: "Ethnic Studies Texts Won't Be in Tucson Classrooms"; "TUSD Banning Books? Well Yes, and No, and Yes"; "Who's Afraid of 'The Tempest'?"[12] The hearing took place in 2013 after officials of the Tucson Unified School District (TUSD) walked into the Mexican American Studies program classrooms and then confiscated

Figure 6.1.   Photo of nine-year-old being wanded by security before the Tucson (Arizona) Unified School District Board Meeting on March 13, 2012. *Robert Rodriguez*

and boxed up textbooks used in the classroom. This was one of the final acts in a long battle to remove the Mexican American Studies (or MAS) from the TUSD curriculum. The MAS in TUSD exists to comply with a 1978 desegregation order from the courts. Ethnic studies classes were added in 1998 to recruit students to TUSD schools, and two outside audits found that the MAS program in particular was beneficial to students. In May of 2010, the Arizona State Legislature passed ARS 15–112, a law specifically crafted to target Tucson's MAS program. The law stated that:

> A school district or charter school in this state shall not include in its program of instruction any courses or classes that include any of the following:
>
> 1. Promote the overthrow of the United States government.
> 2. Promote resentment toward a race or class of people.
> 3. Are designed primarily for pupils of a particular ethnic group.
> 4. Advocate ethnic solidarity instead of the treatment of pupils as individuals. [13]

The TUSD's interpretation of this law led administrators to remove books from the classroom. The cover photograph, by Yolanda Sotelo, is also from this case and shows one of these boxes of books. Under the direction of a district official the books were boxed up, labeled, and placed in the official's car—destined for the local textbook depository. Beyond the grasp of the students who were reading them as part of their Mexican American Studies class. This is knowledge boxed up for disposal—ready to be removed to a place where it can no longer expand the minds of the students possibly leading them to new insights on our society.

The following quote, from an affidavit in the legal case regarding the program, contains language that will now be familiar to the readers of this book: "Curricular materials and text books obtained from TUSD illustrate many examples of lessons that promulgate racial stereotypes, and that insert a kind of poisonous racism in the minds of the students" (Documented facts pertaining to the Ethnic Studies program, sworn testimony at administrative hearing, p. 11). It is hoped that the analysis in this book can help us understand the sometimes inscrutable actions and emotions that surround books, reading, knowledge, and power that result in a nine-year-old boy being wanded for weapons before attending a school board hearing.

NOTES

1. Of course access is not truly ubiquitous—it is easier to have access to books and other information in our society if you are wealthy.

2. More on challengers' sense of community can be found in Norman Poppel and Edwin M. Ashley, "Toward an Understanding of the Censor," *Library Journal* 111, no. 12 (July 1986): 39.

3. Amy Johnson Frykholm, *Rapture Culture: Left Behind in Evangelical America* (New York: Oxford University Press, 2004).

4. For more on apocalypticism in American culture see Frykholm, *Rapture Culture*; and Jason C. Bivins, *Religion of Fear: The Politics of Horror in Conservative Evangelicalism* (New York: Oxford University Press, 2008).

5. For an analysis of traditional gender roles and current discourse surrounding them see *The Way We Really Are: Coming to Terms with America's Changing Families* (New York: Basic, 1998), and *The Way We Never Were: American Families and the Nostalgia Trap* (New York: Basic, 2000), both by Stephanie Coontz.

6. Geoffrey C. Bowker and Susan Leigh Star, *Sorting Things Out: Classification and Its Consequences* (Cambridge, MA: MIT Press, 1999), 297.

7. I could find no evidence of this particular policy on the T. B. Scott Free Library (Merrill, WI) website (http://wvls.lib.wi.us/merrillpl/).

8. For more on the physical layout of the library and the use of sections as a proxy for safety in the library see Emily J. M. Knox, "The Challengers of West Bend: The Library as a Community Institution," in *Libraries and the Reading Public in Twentieth-Century America*, ed. Christine Pawley and Louise S. Robbins (Madison: University of Wisconsin Press, 2013), 200–16.

9. American Library Association, *Intellectual Freedom Manual*, 8th ed. (Chicago: American Library Association, 2010), 155.

10. George Dessart, "Standards and Practices," *Encyclopedia of Television*, 1997, http://www.museum.tv/eotvsection.php?entrycode=standardsand.

11. It is also interesting to think about the importance of short-term effects to challengers' arguments when it comes to challenges to erotica in, for example, the case of *50 Shades of Grey*.

12. Associated Press, "Ethnic Studies Texts Won't Be in Tucson Classrooms," *Arizona Capitol Times*, July 25, 2012, accessed May 29, 2014, http://azcapitoltimes.com/news/2012/07/25/ethnic-studies-texts-wont-be-in-tucson-classrooms/; Mari Herreras, "TUSD Banning Books? Well Yes, and No, and Yes," *Tucson Weekly*, January 17, 2012, accessed May 29, 2014, http://www.tucsonweekly.com/TheRange/archives/2012/01/17/tusd-banning-book-well-yes-and-no-and-yes"; Jeff Biggers, "Who's Afraid of 'The Tempest'?" *Salon*, January 13, 2012, accessed May 29, 2014, http://www.salon.com/2012/01/13/whos_afraid_of_the_tempest/.

13. Arizona State Legislature, *Prohibited Courses and Classes; Enforcement*, n.d., http://www.azleg.gov/FormatDocument.asp?inDoc=/ars/15/00112.htm&Title=15&DocType=ARS.

Source References

BEDFORD, NEW HAMPSHIRE

Male speaker #5. Book challenge hearing. Bedford, NH, February 28, 2011

CARROLLTON, TEXAS

Interview with challenger. Carrollton, TX, January 3, 2012

CENTRAL YORK, PENNSYLVANIA

Interview with challenger. Central York, PA, December 7, 2011

CLARKSTOWN, NEW YORK

Request for reconsideration #1. Clarkstown, NY, date redacted [February 2011]
Female speaker #5. Book challenge hearing. Clarkstown, NY, March 24, 2011
Female speaker #6. Book challenge hearing. Clarkstown, NY, March 24, 2011
Female speaker #8. Book challenge hearing. Clarkstown, NY, March 24, 2011
Male speaker #3. Book challenge hearing. Clarkstown, NY, March 24, 2011
Male speaker #4. Book challenge hearing. Clarkstown, NY, March 24, 2011
Male speaker #6. Book challenge hearing. Clarkstown, NY, March 24, 2011

CONWAY, SOUTH CAROLINA

Female speaker #1. Book challenge hearing. Conway, SC, December 2, 2010

GREENSBORO, NORTH CAROLINA

Request for reconsideration. Greensboro, NC, November 8, 2010

HELENA, MONTANA

Letter to the board. Helena, MT, n.d.
Letter to the board. Helena, MT, December 3, 2010
Interview with challenger. Helena, MT, December 12, 2011
Request for reconsideration. Helena, MT, October 28, 2010

LEWISTON, MAINE

Letter to the board. Lewiston, ME, August 20, 2007
Book challenge letter. Lewiston, ME, January 30, 2008

MERRILL, WISCONSIN

Male speaker #1. Book challenge hearing. Merrill, WI, September 29, 2011
Male speaker #6. Book challenge hearing. Merrill, WI, September 29, 2011
Female speaker #2. Book challenge hearing. Merrill, WI, September 29, 2011
Female speaker #3. Book challenge hearing. Merrill, WI, September 29, 2011
Female speaker #6. Book challenge hearing. Merrill, WI, September 29, 2011
Female speaker #7. Book challenge hearing. Merrill, WI, September 29, 2011
Female speaker #11. Book challenge hearing. Merrill, WI, September 29, 2011
Letter to the board. Merrill, WI, June 10, 2011
Letter to the board. Merrill, WI, June 13, 2011
Letter to the board. Merrill, WI, June 15, 2011
Letter to the board. Merrill, WI, September 27, 2011
Request for reconsideration. Merrill, WI, May 31, 2011
Request for reconsideration. Merrill, WI, June 7, 2011
Request for reconsideration. Merrill, WI, June 11, 2011

Request for reconsideration. Merrill, WI, June 13, 2011
Request for reconsideration. Merrill, WI, June 15, 2011

RANDLEMAN, NORTH CAROLINA

Interview with D. Matthews. October 9, 2013
Interview with T. Boyles. September 27, 2013
Request for reconsideration. Randleman, NC, July 30, 2013
Reconsideration appeal. Randleman, NC, received August 13, 2013
Central Services Committee Report. Randleman, NC, August 13, 2013

SEATTLE, WASHINGTON

Letter to the board. Seattle, WA, March 14, 2010
Letter to the board. Seattle, WA, August 23, 2010

SPRING HILL, FLORIDA

Request for reconsideration. Spring Hill, FL, November 10, 2010

STOCKTON, MISSOURI

Male speaker #1. Book challenge hearing. Stockton, MO, September 8, 2010
Male speaker #3. Book challenge hearing. Stockton, MO, September 8, 2010
Male speaker #4. Book challenge hearing. Stockton, MO, September 8, 2010
Male Speaker #5. Book challenge hearing. Stockton, MO, September 8, 2010
Male speaker #6. Book challenge hearing. Stockton, MO, September 8, 2010
Male speaker #8. Book challenge hearing. Stockton, MO, September 8, 2010
Male speaker #9. Book challenge hearing. Stockton, MO, September 8, 2010
Letter to the board. Stockton, MO, May 10, 2010
Letter to the board. Stockton, MO, May 13, 2010

WESTFIELD, NEW JERSEY

Female speaker #5. Book challenge hearing. Westfield, NJ, February 28, 2012
Male speaker #1. Book challenge hearing. Westfield, NJ, February 28, 2012

Appendix A

Methodological Note

FINDING THE CASES

This appendix presents an overview of the method of data collection and analysis employed in the study. One aspect of the study that required a lot of care was identifying past and current book challenges in public libraries and schools. Since these institutions are supported by public funds, it is often in the interest of their administrators to keep any controversy, including book challenges, out of the public eye. The ALA's Office for Intellectual Freedom (OIF) collects annual statistics on book challenges, but this information is not shared with the public.[1] In keeping with their stated policy, my requests for demographic information regarding challenges to the OIF were denied. I was informed that "we are not able to give our raw data on our challenges because the majority of them are protected by a confidentiality agreement that prohibits us from divulging any identifying information."[2] This meant that I had to take a different approach to finding out about challenge cases.

I employed several methods to identify challenge cases for this study. First, I followed the OIF's news-only e-mail list, IFACTION. Information regarding challenges from various news sources as well as general intellectual freedom materials are posted to the list several times a week. Second, I created several Google Alerts that were set to deliver what the service calls "Everything" including Google web, blog, and news searches. Google-defined "Best Results" were sent to my e-mail approximately once per day. The search terms included various combinations of the following terms: library, board, public, book, challenge, complaint, hearing, banned, censorship, and comment. The final list of general Google Alerts appears at the end of this appendix. If I discovered an item of interest concerning a challenge case through either IFACTION or the Google Alerts, I immediately created a new "As It Happens" Google Alert for the challenge. These alerts included search terms that directly related to the particular case such as the name of the challenged book and location of the challenge. I've included a list of specific challenge case Google Alerts in this appendix as well. I also mentioned the study to any librarians I happened to meet and encouraged them to contact me if they became aware of challenges in their own or another library.

All the challenges found through these methods were entered into a chart consisting of five different spreadsheets: Interviews, Hearings, Groups, More Information Needed, and Consolidated. "Interviews" contained information for challengers I had contacted for interviews and includes columns for notating whether or not I asked them for an interview, his or her acceptance of the request, and other pertinent information. "Hearings" listed information for public challenge hearings including place, date, and whether or not I attended. "Groups" included contact information for local, regional, and national groups that are associated with challengers. "More Information Needed" listed challenges for which there was only a cursory amount of information and, most importantly, lacked the name of the challenger. Finally, the "Consolidated" spreadsheet listed each challenge along with any and all information I had about the case including whether or not I received supporting documentation, possible interviewees, and hearing dates.

After identifying potential challenge cases, I contacted the office of public records for the governing body (generally the school board or municipality) in order to request copies of any and all documents that pertained to the challenge. In order to facilitate the requisition of documents, all the requests cited the state's Freedom of Information Act (FOIA) or Public Records Access laws.[3] The documents often included the name and sometimes contact information for the original complainant. If the original complainant's contact information was readily available, I would request an interview. Finally, if there was a public hearing scheduled, I would determine whether or not it was feasible for me to attend. The three data sources are used as a means of triangulation in order to safeguard the credibility of the study. These data sources are discussed in more detail below.[4]

DOCUMENTS FROM CHALLENGE CASES

Beginning with the initial request for removal or relocation (often called a request for reconsideration; see appendix B), the institutionalized challenge procedure produces a large number of documents. These include such items as written responses from library and school administrators and staff, written responses from challengers, as well as written responses from legal counsel. Library or public school board members also write responses to challenges that become part of the public record.

Responses to the written requests for documents varied. Out of 13 requests, I received responses from 13 governing bodies. (Documents for the Randleman, North Carolina, and West Bend, Wisconsin, case were posted online.) Two of the bodies replied that they were concerned about the privacy of the challengers and sent only cursory information. Three governing bodies sent full documentation including copies of the binders used by the boards in public hearings. Documents were sent both electronically and in hard copy. Two of the responses included DVDs of the public hearings. Six governing bodies posted all pertinent information, including recordings of public hearings and minutes, to the Internet. Hard-copy documents were scanned and all documents were analyzed by means of qualitative research software.

In order to be included in the final set of challenge cases used in the study, documents needed to include challengers' own voices. This meant that most meeting minutes were excluded as they generally only included paraphrases of arguments. There were several different types of documents included in this data source, including requests for reconsideration (the original complaint forms that initiate the challenge case), letters, and e-mails. In order to keep data to a manageable size, letters to the editor and op-eds in local newspapers, even if they included challengers' own words, were excluded.

Recordings and Observation of Public Hearings

When they are not resolved at an earlier stage in the challenge process, requests to remove or relocate materials in public institutions sometimes result in public hearings. There are two primary types of hearings. The first consists of proceedings that are entirely devoted to discussion regarding the request and are often the final public step in a lengthy dispute process. The hearings are held before the decision makers (usually the school or library board) and members of the public are invited to give comments for a set length of time, generally three to 10 minutes. The second type of hearing is generally held in the course of some other meeting, such as, for example, the regular monthly meeting of the school or library board.

Agendas for these meetings often have time set aside for "public comments" and, when a request for removal or relocation is discussed, members of the public may voice their concerns during this time. Commenters usually have a set amount of time to speak (usually three minutes). Both types of hearings are generally held in public facilities that are open to all members of the public including nonconstituents or people who are not part of the library or school board's district. Although participants in the public hearings testified both for and against the removal or relocation of library materials, this study focused on the testimonies of those who support the request for removal or relocation.

I used two procedures for collecting data from public hearings. The first consisted of using audio or video recordings that were available either on the websites of the administrative bodies of public institutions or were sent to me through the Freedom of Information Act document requests described above. I also attended three public hearings (two of which are included in the final data set) during which I recorded the proceedings and took fieldnotes.[5] These are used to add texture to the analysis in the following chapters by noting the setting and atmosphere of the proceedings.

Interviews

The second source of discourse consisted of interviews with individuals who were substantially involved in the removal or reclassification of materials in libraries. As noted above, information from public records including newspapers and documents received through FOIA requests was used to contact interviewees. The process for contacting potential interviewees evolved over time. I began by contacting challengers via e-mail and cold calls in the fall of

2010, but received no response. I also made one attempt to use snowball sampling using an interviewee from the pilot study described below as a catalyst. This method also received no response. As a result of these response rates, in the summer of 2011, I decided to contact challengers via typewritten, posted letter. I was also concerned that the legalistic language in the initial request increased challengers' hesitation to contact me. The typewritten letter was carefully crafted to lessen the legalistic tone in the initial request e-mail. If a challenger contacted me, either via phone or e-mail, I immediately sent him or her a follow-up letter via e-mail or snail mail and consent forms, which were required by the Institutional Review Boards of my universities. Out of the 38 initial request letters, 12 challengers and one individual who was significantly involved but not a challenger in the Randleman, North Carolina, case contacted me. Of these 12 possible interviewees, five agreed to be interviewed.[6]

The interviews took place over the phone and were audio recorded and transcribed. The questions were designed to invite interviewees to talk at length and reflect on their beliefs and experiences regarding the library in society, reading, and challenges to materials. The interview protocol, which followed a semistructured format, was divided into three question clusters that related to the research objectives and were tailored to the individual interviewee. After an initial overview and introduction, the first cluster included questions regarding how the interviewee understood the practice of reading. The second cluster focused on the library or school (depending on the interviewee) as an institution. The final cluster of questions discussed the actual challenge in which the interviewee was involved.

ANALYSIS AND INTERPRETATION

Discourse Analysis

For the purposes of this study, discourse is defined using Bourdieu's concepts of structured structure and structuring structure. In this social constructionist conceptualization, discourse both provides context for and constructs the social world. It also provides meaning for the objects that one encounters in the social world. In this formulation, discourse can be understood as part of an individual's *habitus*. More specifically, discourse is "an interrelated set of texts and the practices of their production, dissemination, and reception that brings an object into being."[7] Discourse is, of course, created from language, but it is not simply language that exists "outside" of particular individuals but also actionable, that is, "what they do" with the language themselves.

Following the work of Schutz, Berger, and Luckmann, language is considered to be "constitutive of reality."[8] Language does not merely describe the world; it also constructs the objects that exist within it. Following from this, discourse analysis is a methodology wherein the researcher explores how social reality is created through these texts. Following Bourdieu, the analysis reveals both the structuring structures of context and the structured structures of meaning. Through analysis of discourse, the researcher can begin to uncover the social structures of particular worldviews—in the case of this study, the worldviews of challengers. Discourse analysis incorporates an epistemology grounded in social constructionism.

Although there are many different types of discourse analysis, this study takes a culturalist discourse research approach as described by Reiner Keller.[9] As described in chapter 1, this approach is grounded in two foundational theories. The first is symbolic interactionism, which posits that human beings create meaning through interactions with other human beings. Meanings are social products "that are formed in and through the defining activities of people as they interact."[10] It is through the observation of these interactions that researchers can discover culture. Meaning is created through a process of interpretation then shared with others in society, and society cannot exist without these shared meanings that constitute social interaction.

The second major foundation for culturalist discourse research is Bourdieu's theories that investigate how people use language and its interaction with symbolic power. Although these terms were described in some detail in chapter 2, in order to comprehend their relationship to discourse analysis, it is important to understand how Bourdieu uses the term "symbolic systems" to grasp his definition of symbolic power. Symbolic systems are both structuring structures that allow for cognition and structured structures that organize meaning. Bourdieu describes two "syntheses" through which symbols gain power.[11] The first synthesis (a naturalization process that allows for the normalization of symbolic systems) allows for social integration. For example, the use of types allows everyone in a given social system to understand what various objects are in the social world. In the second synthesis, symbolic systems become political through meaning making and cognition. The objects are no longer simply objects of material reality; they now have social meaning and symbolic significance attached to them.

In this latter synthesis, different groups of individuals struggle symbolically in order to impose their own definitions of particular symbols in the social world on others.[12] "Struggles over the specific objects of the autonomous field automatically produce euphemized forms of the economic and political struggles between classes."[13] Most importantly, symbolic power is misrecognized as common sense. The idea of common sense both in a philosophical sense and in terms of textual interpretation is discussed in more detail in chapter 2.

Coding and Interpretation

Data were analyzed with codes for common themes. At the beginning of the analysis, the researcher coded the data on the sentence level. After realizing that the sentences did not provide enough context for the themes, all of the data were coded at approximately the paragraph level (three to five sentences). Paragraphs usually received multiple codes. Conclusions from three pilot studies that I conducted and previous research by Loretta Gaffney and Kelly Kingrey provided an outline for an original coding scheme, which was divided into the following categories: institutions, justifications, power and control, and reading practices. [14]

Coding was an iterative process as it was found that the original classification of codes did not adequately match either the objectives of the study of the arguments of the challengers. The codes were rearranged to more adequately match the study's purpose, and data analysis also continually revealed new codes. These codes were added to the scheme throughout analysis, and previously coded arguments were recoded if needed. The final coding scheme was divided into three categories that correlated with the original research objectives of the studies: worldviews, libraries and other institutions, and reading practices/effects/books. In conclusion, it is hoped that this note clarifies both how the cases were found and analyzed in this study.

GENERAL GOOGLE ALERTS

"library board" meeting OR hearing book
banned book
book "public comment"
book "public hearing"
censorship library
library book hearing OR meeting
library "public hearing" book
library book challenge
library book complaint
library book reconsideration
library committee meeting OR hearing

CASE-SPECIFIC GOOGLE ALERTS

"blue springs school district" "hold still"
"bluest eye" brookfield
"borrowed time" Cheatham School
"columbia county library" mansbach

"dade county" "absolutely true"
"grand rapids" "history alive"
"hold still" "blue springs"
"hunt club" charleston school board
"in cold blood" glendale
"montana 1948" merrill
"my mom's having a baby" carrollton library
"running with the buffaloes"
"stuck in the middle" buckfield
"study in scarlet" albemarle
Arizona hb2563 bible
brookfield "bluest eye"
easton "nickled and dimed"
huffman independent blackburn
kalida lush
knox county "looking for alaska"
pickens county romeo juliet
Plymouth-Canton school board beloved
tangled borger
troy area school board "kite runner"
tucson unified books
westfield book alexie

NOTES

1. From the OIF's website: "Challenges reported to the ALA by individuals are kept confidential. In these cases, ALA will release only the title of the book being challenged, the state and the type of institution (school, public library). The name of the institution and its town will not be disclosed" (http://www.ala.org/advocacy/banned/frequentlychallenged).

2. Personal communication, September 24, 2009.

3. These requests will be noted hereafter as FOIA requests after the federal Freedom of Information Act. Each of the 50 states has its own version of this act (http://www.nfoic.org/state-freedom-of-information-laws).

4. Although the term "data" can be controversial when used in social science research, I am following both Phillips and Hardy and Keller in my use of the term throughout this study. Nelson Phillips and Cynthia Hardy, *Discourse Analysis: Investigating Processes of Social Construction* (Thousand Oaks, CA: Sage, 2002); Reiner Keller, "Analysing Discourse: An Approach from the Sociology of Knowledge," *Forum Qualitative Sozialforschung/Forum: Qualitative Social Research* 6, no. 3 (2005), http://www.qualitative-research.net/index.php/fqs/article/view/19.

5. According to Robert M. Emerson, Rachel I. Fretz, and Linda L. Shaw, "Fieldnotes are products of and reflect conventions for transforming witnessed events, persons, and places into words on paper" (Emerson, Fretz, and Shaw, *Writing Ethnographic Fieldnotes* [Chicago: University of Chicago Press, 1995], p. 9). Writing fieldnotes involves a type of description in which the act of writing is part of the interpretation process and constitutes the first step for "textualizing" the data for the researcher. In keeping with the ethnographic principles of thick description, fieldnotes from the public hearings are used to show the behavior of the participants and not tell it.

6. It is possible that the legalistic tone in the consent forms, as is required by the Institutional Review Board (IRB), concerned many of the possible interviewees. The tone of the forms, in some respects, made the study seem suspicious. One potential interviewee voiced concerns regarding the need to be anonymous. If my study was aboveboard, why could I not use the potential interviewee's name?

7. Phillips and Hardy, *Discourse Analysis*, 3.

8. Phillips and Hardy, *Discourse Analysis*, 12.

9. Keller, "Analysing Discourse."

10. Herbert Blumer, *Symbolic Interactionism: Perspective and Method* (Englewood Cliffs, NJ: Prentice Hall, 1969), 5.

11. Pierre Bourdieu, *Language and Symbolic Power* (Cambridge, MA: Harvard University Press, 1991).

12. Bourdieu, *Language and Symbolic Power*.

13. Bourdieu, *Language and Symbolic Power*, 169.

14. Loretta M. Gaffney, "Intellectual Freedom and the Politics of Reading: Libraries as Sites of Conservative Activism, 1990–2010" (PhD diss., University of Illinois at Urbana-Champaign, 2012); Kelly Kingrey, "Perceptions of Intellectual Freedom among Conservative Christian Advocacy Groups: A Grounded Theory Analysis" (PhD diss., Texas Woman's University, 2005).

Appendix B

Sample Request for Reconsideration

The school board of Mainstream County, U.S.A., has delegated the responsibility for selection and evaluation of library/educational resources to the school library media specialist/curriculum committee, and has established reconsideration procedures to address concerns about those resources. Completion of this form is the first step in those procedures. If you wish to request reconsideration of school or library resources, please return the completed form to the Coordinator of Library Media Resources, Mainstream School Dist., 1 Mainstream Plaza, Anytown, U.S.A.

Name _____

Date _____

Address _____

City _____

State _____

Zip _____

Phone _____

Do you represent self? ____ Organization? ____

1. Resource on which you are commenting:

    ____ Book ____ Textbook ____ Video ____ Display ____ Magazine ____ Library Program
    ____ Audio Recording ____ Newspaper ____ Electronic information/network (please specify)
    ____ Other _____
    Title _____
    Author/Producer _____

2. What brought this resource to your attention?
3. Have you examined the entire resource?
4. What concerns you about the resource? (use other side or additional pages if necessary)
5. Are there resource(s) you suggest to provide additional information and/or other viewpoints on this topic?

Revised by the American Library Association Intellectual Freedom Committee

June 27, 1995

Source: http://www.ala.org/advocacy/banned/challengeslibrarymaterials/copingwithchallenges/samplereconsideration

Appendix C

Chart of Challenge Cases

ace	Date	Challenged Institution	Challenged Material	Documents	Hearing	Intervi
edford, NH	2011	Bedford Board of Education	*Water for Elephants*	Yes	Yes	No
arrollton, TX	2011	Carrollton Board of Education	*My Mom's Having a Baby*	Yes	No	Yes
entral York, A	2010	Central York School District	*Stolen Children*	No	No	Yes
arkstown, Y	2011	Clarkstown Board of Education	*The Perks of Being a Wallflower*	Yes	Yes	No
onway, SC	2011	Horry County Board of Education	*Push*	Yes	Yes	No
reensboro, C	2010	Guilford County Board of Education	*Hoops*	Yes	No	No
elena, MT	2010	Helena School District	*The Absolutely True Diary of a Part-Time Indian*	Yes	Yes	Yes
ewiston, ME	2007	Lewiston PL	*It's Perfectly Normal*	Yes	No	No
errlll, WI	2011	Merrill Area Public Schools	*Montana 1948*	Yes	Yes	No
andleman, C	2013	Randolph County Public Schools	*Invisible Man*	Yes	Yes	Yes
eattle, WA	2010	Seattle Board of Education	*Brave New World*	Yes	No	No
pring Hill, L	2010	Hernando County Board of Education	*Snakehead*	Yes	No	No
tockton, MO	2010	Stockton School District	*The Absolutely True Diary of a Part-Time Indian*	Yes	Yes	No

| | Bend, | 2009 | West Bend Public Library | Various | Yes | Yes | No |
| | field, NJ | 2012 | Westfield Public Schools | *The Absolutely True Diary of a Part-Time Indian* | No | Yes | No |

Bibliography

American Library Association. "Frequently Challenged Books of the 21st Century." N.d. http://www.ala.org/bbooks/frequentlychallengedbooks/top10.

———. "Intellectual Freedom and Censorship Q & A." N.d. http://www.ala.org/Template.cfm?Section=basics&Template=/ContentManagement/ContentDisplay.cfm&ContentID=60610.

———. *Intellectual Freedom Manual.* 8th ed. Chicago: American Library Association, 2010.

American Library Association Office for Intellectual Freedom. "Most Frequently Challenged Authors of the 21st Century." Accessed July 22, 2014. http://www.ala.org/bbooks/frequentlychallengedbooks/challengedauthors.

Arizona State Legislature. *Prohibited Courses and Classes; Enforcement.* N.d. http://www.azleg.gov/FormatDocument.asp?inDoc=/ars/15/00112.htm&Title=15&DocType=ARS.

Associated Press. "Ethnic Studies Texts Won't Be in Tucson Classrooms." *Arizona Capitol Times*, July 25, 2012. Accessed May 29, 2014. http://azcapitoltimes.com/news/2012/07/25/ethnic-studies-texts-wont-be-in-tucson-classrooms/.

Atkin, Albert. "Peirce's Theory of Signs." In *The Stanford Encyclopedia of Philosophy*, edited by Edward N. Zalta, Summer 2013 ed. http://plato.stanford.edu/archives/sum2013/entries/peirce-semiotics/.

Beisel, Nicola. *Imperiled Innocents: Anthony Comstock and Family Reproduction in Victorian America.* Princeton, NJ: Princeton University Press, 1997.

Berger, Peter L., and Thomas Luckmann. *The Social Construction of Reality.* New York: Anchor, 1966.

Biggers, Jeff. "Who's Afraid of 'The Tempest'?" *Salon*, January 13, 2012. Accessed May 29, 2014. http://www.salon.com/2012/01/13/whos_afraid_of_the_tempest/.

Bivins, Jason C. *Religion of Fear: The Politics of Horror in Conservative Evangelicalism.* New York: Oxford University Press, 2008.

Blumer, Herbert. *Symbolic Interactionism: Perspective and Method.* Englewood Cliffs, NJ: Prentice Hall, 1969.

Boggioni, Tom. "Concerned Idaho Citizen Calls Police over Public Banned Book Giveaway to High School Students." *Raw Story*, April 27, 2014. Accessed May 15, 2014. http://www.rawstory.com/rs/2014/04/27/concerned-idaho-citizen-calls-police-over-public-banned-book-giveaway-to-high-school-students/.

Bonfil, Robert. "Reading in the Jewish Communities of Western Europe in the Middle Ages." In *A History of Reading in the West*, edited by Guglielmo Cavallo and Roger Chartier, 149–78. Amherst: University of Massachusetts Press, 2003.

Bourdieu, Pierre. "The Forms of Capital." In *Handbook of Theory and Research for the Sociology of Education*, edited by John G. Richardson, 241–58. Westport, CT: Greenwood, 1986.

————. *Language and Symbolic Power.* Cambridge, MA: Harvard University Press, 1991.

————. *Outline of a Theory of Practice.* New York: Cambridge University Press, 1987.

————. "Social Space and Symbolic Power." *Sociological Theory* 7, no. 1 (Spring 1989): 14–25.

————. "The Social Space and the Genesis of Groups." *Theory and Society* 14, no. 6 (1985): 723–44.

Bowker, Geoffrey C., and Susan Leigh Star. *Sorting Things Out: Classification and Its Consequences.* Cambridge, MA: MIT Press, 1999.

Burke, Peter. *A Social History of Knowledge: From Gutenberg to Diderot, Based on the First Series of Vonhoff Lectures Given at the University of Groningen (Netherlands).* Malden, MA: Polity, 2000.

Chartier, Roger. "The Practical Impact of Writing." In *The Book History Reader*, edited by David Finkelstein and Alistair McCleery, 157–81. New York: Routledge, 2002.

Colclough, Stephen. *Consuming Texts: Readers and Reading Communities, 1695–1870.* New York: Palgrave Macmillan, 2007.

Coontz, Stephanie. *The Way We Never Were: American Families and the Nostalgia Trap.* New York: Basic, 2000.

————. *The Way We Really Are: Coming to Terms with America's Changing Families.* New York: Basic, 1998.

Craig, Maureen A., and Jennifer A. Richeson. "On the Precipice of a 'Majority-Minority' America: Perceived Status Threat from the Racial Demographic Shift Affects White Americans' Political Ideology." *Psychological Science*, April 3, 2014. doi:10.1177/0956797614527113.

Darnton, Robert. *The Business of Enlightenment: A Publishing History of the 'Encyclopédie,' 1775–1800.* Cambridge, MA: Belknap, 1979.

Davidson, Cathy. *Revolution and the Word: The Rise of the Novel in America.* Expanded ed. New York: Oxford University Press, 2004.

Dessart, George. "Standards and Practices." *Encyclopedia of Television*, 1997. http://www.museum.tv/eotvsection.php?entrycode=standardsand.

Doyle, Robert P. *Banned Books: Challenging Our Freedom to Read.* Chicago: American Library Association, 2010.

Dresang, Eliza T. "Intellectual Freedom and Libraries: Complexity and Change in the Twenty-First-Century Digital Environment." *Library Quarterly* 76, no. 2 (April 1, 2006): 169–92. doi:10.1086/506576.

Dworkin, Andrea, and Catharine A. MacKinnon. *Pornography and Civil Rights: A New Day for Women's Equality.* Minneapolis, MN: Organizing Against Pornography, 1988.

Eisenstein, Elizabeth L. *The Printing Revolution in Early Modern Europe.* 2nd ed. Cambridge, UK: Cambridge University Press, 2005.

Emerson, Robert M., Rachel I. Fretz, and Linda L. Shaw, *Writing Ethnographic Fieldnotes.* Chicago: University of Chicago Press, 1995.

Finkelstein, David, and Alistair McCleery. *An Introduction to Book History.* New York: Routledge, 2005.

Fish, Stanley Eugene. *Is There a Text in This Class?* Cambridge, MA: Harvard University Press, 1982.

Fishburn, Matthew. *Burning Books.* New York: Palgrave Macmillan, 2008.

Frykholm, Amy Johnson. *Rapture Culture: Left Behind in Evangelical America.* New York: Oxford University Press, 2004.

G., Jessica. "Remember That Wisconsin Woman Arrested for Overdue Books?" *Jezebel* (blog), August 28, 2008. Accessed July 24, 2014. http://jezebel.com/5043035/.

Gaffney, Loretta M. "Intellectual Freedom and the Politics of Reading: Libraries as Sites of Conservative Activism, 1990–2010." PhD diss., University of Illinois at Urbana-Champaign, 2012.

Gilmont, Lydia G. "Reading and the Counter-Reformation." In *A History of Reading in the West*, edited by Guglielmo Cavallo and Roger Chartier, 238–68. Amherst: University of Massachusetts Press, 2003.

Gilmore, William J. *Reading Becomes a Necessity of Life: Material and Cultural Life in Rural New England, 1780–1835*. Knoxville: University of Tennessee Press, 1989.

Gonzales, Eric. "Meridian Police Show Up to Free Book Giveaway." *KBOI 2 News*, April 23, 2014. Accessed May 12, 2014. http://www.kboi2.com/news/local/Meridian-police-show-up-to-free-book-giveaway--256475781.html.

Grafton, Anthony. "The Humanist as Reader." In *A History of Reading in the West*, edited by Guglielmo Cavallo and Roger Chartier, 179–212. Amherst: University of Massachusetts Press, 2003.

Gutjahr, Paul C. "No Longer Left Behind: Amazon.com, Reader Response, and the Changing Fortunes of the Christian Novel in America." *Book History*, 2002, 209–36.

Hamesse, Jacqueline. "The Scholastic Model of Reading." In *A History of Reading in the West*, edited by Guglielmo Cavallo and Roger Chartier, 103–19. Amherst: University of Massachusetts Press, 2003.

Herreras, Mari. "TUSD Banning Books? Well Yes, and No, and Yes." *Tucson Weekly*, January 17, 2012. Accessed May 29, 2014. http://www.tucsonweekly.com/TheRange/archives/2012/01/17/tusd-banning-book-well-yes-and-no-and-yes.

Hunter, James Davison. *Culture Wars: The Struggle to Control the Family, Art, Education, Law, and Politics in America*. New York: Basic, 1992.

Jansen, Sue Curry. *Censorship: The Knot That Binds Power and Knowledge*. New York: Oxford University Press, 1988.

Jardine, Lisa. "The Triumph of the Book." In *Worldly Goods*, 135–80. New York: Norton, 1998.

Jenkins, Christine A. "Book Challenges, Challenging Books, and Young Readers: The Research Picture." *Language Arts* 85, no. 3 (2008): 228.

Johns, Adrian. *The Nature of the Book: Print and Knowledge in the Making*. 1st ed. Chicago: University of Chicago Press, 2000.

Jones, Barbara M., and American Library Association Office for Intellectual Freedom. *Protecting Intellectual Freedom in Your Academic Library: Scenarios from the Front Lines*. Chicago: American Library Association, 2009.

Keller, Reiner. "Analysing Discourse: An Approach from the Sociology of Knowledge." *Forum Qualitative Sozialforschung/Forum: Qualitative Social Research* 6, no. 3 (2005). http://www.qualitative-research.net/index.php/fqs/article/view/19.

Keys, Kathi. "Board to Reconsider Its 'Invisible Man' Ban." *Asheboro (NC) Courier-Tribune*. September 19, 2013. http://courier-tribune.com/sections/news/local/board-reconsider-its-%E2%80%98invisible-man%E2%80%99-ban.html.

———. "County Board Bans 'Invisible Man' from School Libraries." *Asheboro (NC) Courier-Tribune*. September 16, 2013. http://courier-tribune.com/sections/news/local/county-board-bans-%E2%80%98invisible-man%E2%80%99-school-libraries.html.

Kingrey, Kelly. "Perceptions of Intellectual Freedom among Conservative Christian Advocacy Groups: A Grounded Theory Analysis." PhD diss., Texas Woman's University, 2005.

Knox, Emily J. M. "The Books Will Still Be in the Library: Narrow Definitions of Censorship in the Discourse of Challengers." *Library Trends* 62, no. 4 (2014).

———. "The Challengers of West Bend: The Library as a Community Institution." In *Libraries and the Reading Public in Twentieth-Century America*, edited by Christine Pawley and Louise S. Robbins, 200–16. Madison: University of Wisconsin Press, 2013.

———. "Intellectual Freedom and the Agnostic-Postmodern View of Reading Effects." *Library Trends* 63, no. 1 (2014).

———. "Supporting Intellectual Freedom: Symbolic Capital and Practical Philosophy in Librarianship." *Library Quarterly* 84, no. 1 (2014): 1–14.

Knuth, Rebecca. *Burning Books and Leveling Libraries: Extremist Violence and Cultural Destruction*. Westport, CT: Greenwood, 2006.

Kohl, Herbert R. *Should We Burn Babar? Essays on Children's Literature and the Power of Stories*. New York: New Press, 1995. Distributed by Norton.

Kromm, Chris, and Sue Sturgis. "North Carolina's Tug-of-War." *American Prospect*, June 6, 2013. http://prospect.org/article/north-carolinas-tug-war.

LaRue, James. *The New Inquisition: Understanding and Managing Intellectual Freedom Challenges*. Westport, CT: Libraries Unlimited, 2007.

Long, Elizabeth. "Textual Interpretation as Collective Action." In *The Ethnography of Reading*, edited by J. Boyarin, 180–211. Berkeley: University of California Press, 1992.

Lor, Peter Johan, and Johannes Jacobus Britz. "Is a Knowledge Society Possible without Freedom of Access to Information?" *Journal of Information Science* 33, no. 4 (August 1, 2007): 387–97. doi:10.1177/0165551506075327.

Lyons, Martyn. *A History of Reading and Writing in the Western World*. New York: Palgrave Macmillan, 2010.

Marsden, George. *Understanding Fundamentalism and Evangelicalism*. Grand Rapids, MI: Eerdmans, 1991.

Maton, Karl. "Habitus." In *Pierre Bourdieu: Key Concepts*, edited by Michael Grenfell, 49–66. Durham, UK: Acumen, 2008.

Mayer, Jane. "State for Sale." *New Yorker*, October 10, 2011. http://www.newyorker.com/reporting/2011/10/10/111010fa_fact_mayer?currentPage=all.

Mill, John Stuart. *On Liberty*. Indianapolis: Hackett, 1978.

Miller, Alyson. "Unsuited for Age Group: The Scandals of Children's Literature." *College Literature: A Journal of Critical Literary Studies* 41, no. 2 (April 1, 2014): 120–40.

Mullin, Robert. *A Short World History of Christianity*. Louisville, KY: Westminster John Knox Press, 2008.

National Governors Association and Council of Chief State School Officers. "Common Core State Standards for English Language Arts & Literacy in History/Social Studies, Science, and Technical Subjects: Appendix B: Text Exemplars and Sample Performance Tasks." 2010. www.corestandards.org/assets/Appendix_B.pdf.

Noll, Mark. *America's God: From Jonathan Edwards to Abraham Lincoln*. New York: Oxford University Press, 2002.

North Carolina Department of Public Instruction. "Instructional Support Tools for Achieving New Standards: Essential Standards: American Humanities: Unpacked Content." North Carolina Department of Public Instruction, March 9, 2012. http://www.ncpublicschools.org/docs/acre/standards/support-tools/unpacking/social-studies/american-humanities.pdf.

North Carolina State Board of Education. "Randleman High School Report Card: 2012–2013." http://www.ncreportcards.org/src/schDetails.jsp?pYear=2012-2013&pLEACode=760&pSchCode=348.

Nye, Valerie, and Kathy Barco. *True Stories of Censorship Battles in America's Libraries*. Chicago: American Library Association, 2012.

Parkes, M. B. "Reading, Copying and Interpreting a Text in the Early Middle Ages." In *A History of Reading in the West*, edited by Guglielmo Cavallo and Roger Chartier, 90–102. Amherst: University of Massachusetts Press, 2003.

Petley, Julian. *Censorship: A Beginner's Guide*. Oxford: Oneworld, 2009.

Phillips, Nelson, and Cynthia Hardy. *Discourse Analysis: Investigating Processes of Social Construction*. Thousand Oaks, CA: Sage, 2002.

Pinnell-Stephens, June, and American Library Association Office for Intellectual Freedom. *Protecting Intellectual Freedom in Your Public Library: Scenarios from the Front Lines*. Chicago: American Library Association, 2012.

Poppel, Norman, and Edwin M. Ashley. "Toward an Understanding of the Censor." *Library Journal* 111, no. 12 (July 1986): 39–43.

Price, Leah. "Reading: The State of the Discipline." *Book History* 7 (2004): 303–20.

Randolph County NAACP. "To Randolph County Board of Education." September 24, 2013. https://www.facebook.com/permalink.php?story_fbid=394654647328215&id=117164218410594.

Randolph County Schools. "Central Services Committee Report." August 13, 2013. https://www.documentcloud.org/documents/798235-invisible-man-parents-complaint.html.

———. "Request for Reconsideration of Instructional Media." July 31, 2013. https://www.documentcloud.org/documents/798235-invisible-man-parents-complaint.html.

———. "School-Based Committee Report." August 6, 2013. https://www.documentcloud.org/documents/798235-invisible-man-parents-complaint.html.

Robbins, Louise S. *The Dismissal of Miss Ruth Brown: Civil Rights, Censorship, and the American Library*. Norman: University of Oklahoma Press, 2001.

Roberts, Bill. "The Absolutely True Story of What Happened to That Book in Meridian." *Idaho Statesman*, April 2, 2014. Accessed May 12, 2014. http://www.idahostatesman.com/2014/ 04/02/3114247/the-absolutely-true-story-of-what.html.

Robinson, Kerry H. *Innocence, Knowledge, and the Construction of Childhood: The Contradictory Nature of Sexuality and Censorship in Children's Contemporary Lives*. London: Routledge, 2013.

Roiphe, Katie. "It Was, Like, All Dark and Stormy." *Wall Street Journal*, June 6, 2009, sec. News.http://online.wsj.com/news/articles/SB10001424052970203771904574173403357 573642.

Rubel, Alan. "Libraries, Electronic Resources, and Privacy: The Case for Positive Intellectual Freedom." *Library Quarterly* 84, no. 2 (April 2014): 183–208. doi:10.1086/675331.

Saenger, Paul. "Reading in the Later Middle Ages." In *A History of Reading in the West*, edited by Guglielmo Cavallo and Roger Chartier, 102–48. Amherst: University of Massachusetts Press, 2003.

Scales, Pat, and American Library Association Office for Intellectual Freedom. *Protecting Intellectual Freedom in Your School Library: Scenarios from the Front Lines*. Chicago: American Library Association, 2009.

Schutz, Alfred, and Thomas Luckmann. *The Structures of the Life-World*. Evanston, IL: Northwestern University Press, 1973.

Segrest, Scott Philip. *America and the Political Philosophy of Common Sense*. Columbia: University of Missouri Press, 2010.

Seiter, Ellen. "Semiotics, Structuralism, and Television." In *Channels of Discourse, Reassembled: Television and Contemporary Criticism*, edited by Robert C. Allen, 31–66. 2nd ed. Chapel Hill: University of North Carolina Press, 1992.

Selcer, Daniel. *Philosophy and the Book: Early Modern Figures of Material Inscription*. New York: Continuum, 2010.

Stallybrass, Peter. "Visible and Invisible Letters: Text versus Image in Renaissance England and Europe." In *Visible Writings: Cultures, Forms, Readings*, edited by Marija Dalbello and Mary Lewis Shaw, 77–98. New Brunswick, NJ: Rutgers University Press, 2011.

Stock, Brian. *Listening for the Text*. Baltimore: Johns Hopkins University Press, 1996.

Thompson, Bill. "County Library Shuns '50 Shades of Grey.'" *Ocala (FL) Star-Banner*, May 15, 2012. http://docs.newsbank.com.proxy2.library.illinois.edu/s/InfoWeb/aggdocs/AWNB/ 13ED04E00DD58100/0D0CB57DF8A1C275?s_lang.

United Nations. The Universal Declaration of Human Rights. Accessed July 16, 2014. http:// www.un.org/en/documents/udhr/.

Walsh, Sean Collins. "Seattle School Board Postpones Decision on Pulling 'Brave New World.'" *Seattle Times*, November 17, 2010. Accessed July 16, 2014. http://seattletimes. com/html/localnews/2013460397_braveworld18m.html.

Warner, Michael. "Publics and Counterpublics." *Public Culture* 14, no. 1 (2002): 49–90.

Wiegand, Shirley A., and Wayne A. Wiegand. *Books on Trial: Red Scare in the Heartland*. Norman: University of Oklahoma Press, 2007.

Wiegand, Wayne A. "MisReading LIS Education." *Library Journal* 122, no. 11 (1997): 36–38.

———. "Tunnel Vision and Blind Spots: What the Past Tells Us about the Present; Reflections on the Twentieth-Century History of American Librarianship." *Library Quarterly* 69, no. 1 (1999): 1–32.

Zoom, Doktor. "Derp Roundup: Idaho Parents Call Cops to Protect Children from Banned Book." *Wonkette*, April 26, 2014. Accessed May 12, 2014. http://wonkette.com/547677/ derp-roundup-idaho-parents-call-cops-to-protect-children-from-banned-book#K3LderIEXU4AHUPO.99.

Index

CPSIA information can be obtained
at www.ICGtesting.com
Printed in the USA
LVHW042038190323
741983LV00003B/508

About the Author

Emily J. M. Knox is an assistant professor in the Graduate School of Library and Information Science at the University of Illinois at Urbana-Champaign. She received her doctoral degree from the Department of Library and Information Science at the Rutgers University School of Communication and Information. Her research interests include intellectual freedom and censorship, the intersection of print culture and reading practices, and information ethics and policy. She has published several articles and chapters on intellectual freedom.